On Eponymy in Economics
and Other Essays

On Eponymy in Economics
and Other Essays

Julio H. Cole

J & G Ediciones

Guatemala

ISBN: 978-0-9980130-7-7

For Alice and Celine

Contents

Preface   xi

Foreword by Gustavo A. Prado Robles   xiii

I. EPONYMY IN ECONOMICS

1. On Eponymy in Economics   3

II. THE CASE FOR ECONOMIC FREEDOM

2. The False Promise of Protectionism for Latin America   21

3. The Contribution of Economic Freedom to World Economic Growth   41

4. Handling Economic Freedom in Growth Regressions: Suggestions for Clarification (with Robert A. Lawson)   53

III. THE UNEASY CASE FOR PATENTS AND COPYRIGHTS

5. Patents and Copyrights: Do the Benefits Exceed the Costs?   63

Addendum — Review of *The Global Governance of Knowledge*, by Peter Drahos   89

IV. STUDIES ON MILTON FRIEDMAN

6. Milton Friedman, 1912-2006   97

7. Milton Friedman on Income Inequality   117

Addendum — Review of *Milton Friedman*, by William Ruger   133

APPENDIX — SHORTER COMMENTS AND REVIEWS

A. Review of *Just Get Out of the Way: How*   139
    Government Can Help Business in Poor Countries,
    by Robert E. Anderson

B. Review of *The Collected Works of Arthur Seldon,*   143
    vol. 1: *The Virtues of Capitalism*

C. Foreword to *Ensayos de Historia Económica,*   147
    by Gustavo A. Prado Robles

D. In Memoriam: Joseph E. Keckeissen, 1925-2011   149

E. The Achievement of Arnold Harberger   153

PUBLICATIONS BY JULIO H. COLE   161

PREFACE

The essays and papers collected in this volume represent a fair sampling of my views on some of the main themes and research topics that have held my professional attention over the past three decades. Whether the results justify the time and effort that I devoted to these studies is something that my dear readers must decide for themselves. As for myself, I enjoyed writing each and every one of them, and I cannot think of any better use of the time I spent working on them.

In preparing these papers for republication, I could not let pass the opportunity to undo some of the stylistic and editorial changes introduced by the editors of the different publications in which they originally appeared. Though I greatly appreciate their efforts to improve the quality of my presentations and the clarity of my prose, I nonetheless decided, for the most part, to go with my original versions, so in several cases some major deletions have been silently restored, and many minor editorial changes have been discreetly undone. I did, however, resist the temptation to correct errors or omissions in the original papers, or otherwise upgrade or update them. In terms of content, they are essentially reprinted here as originally written.

Finally, I am grateful to my UFM colleague, Dr. Moris Polanco, for his valuable help in preparing this book for publication, and to my fellow economist, Prof. Gustavo Prado Robles, for his generous foreword. As editor of *Revista de Humanidades y Ciencias Sociales*, Gustavo published Spanish-language versions of several of these papers over the years, and he has always been a kind and sympathetic supporter of my researches in many different fields. To both of my good friends, many thanks.

J. H. C.
Guatemala, 2017

FOREWORD

My first encounter with Professor Julio Cole happened two decades ago in Santa Cruz, Bolivia. He had been invited to teach Econometrics at the Universidad Privada de Santa Cruz, and I was a Professor of Economic History and director of the Institute for Economic and Social Research in the School of Economics at Universidad Autónoma "Gabriel René Moreno". We were introduced by Professor Marco Antonio del Río, a mutual friend and colleague who taught at both universities. Since our first meeting, I was impressed by his vast culture as well as by his gentle manners. We began to meet regularly to talk about economics and economic history, and naturally became close friends. In 1999 Julio returned to Universidad Francisco Marroquín, in Guatemala, as the director of the Ludwig von Mises Library and Professor of Economics, but he always took the time to keep in touch and he would often send me the results of his new academic research. As editor of the *Revista de Humanidades y Ciencias Sociales*, I had the privilege of publishing Spanish versions of eight articles of his authorship between 1997 and 2013.

Julio once told me, a long time ago, that as a teenager he considered seriously to become an entomologist. Knowing his intellectual aptitudes, I am sure he would have excelled as a professional in any field of study he had pursued, though I celebrate, of course, the fact that he inclined towards economics. Julio decided to be an economist due to Arnold Harberger's charismatic influence, but he became the notable economist he is today thanks to Milton Friedman's inspiration.[1]

Julio Cole is a free thinker with a curious, systematic and creative mind. His intellectual interests are not confined to diverse subfields of economic theory and quantitative methods. He is also well read in history and literature. The wide range of his scientific and humanistic research interests is impressive. Over the years, he has conducted extensive scholarly research in monetary issues, economic growth, economic foundations of patents and copyrights, and the history of economic

---

[1] Julio recalls that it was while attending a lecture by Professor Arnold Harberger, as an undergraduate student, that he probably took the final decision of becoming an economist (p. 155). After reading his remarkable obituary for Milton Friedman (especially pp. 110-11), one can certainly understand the great inspiring influence that the world-famous economist (and reportedly wonderful human being) personally had on Julio during his early years as a young academic.

thought, with a special concentration on the work of prominent liberal thinkers, such as Adam Smith and Milton Friedman. More recently, his essays on the liberal ideas of celebrated novelists, such as Mario Vargas Llosa and George Orwell, have been awarded important prizes in international literary contests. Cole is a *rara avis* among contemporary academic economists, who are often constrained by overspecialization and face the risk of knowing *more and more about less and less*.

He openly proclaims his adherence to the principles of a free society, but he is not unwilling (in fact, quite willing) to show specific disagreements, even with very prominent liberal scholars, when he considers it is pertinent. His criticisms are always relevant, well founded and carefully expounded, and he is rigorous and respectful in questioning accepted wisdom as well as generous in praising the merits of knowledge achieved by means of good scientific practices and procedures.

He also writes with clarity and grace. He approaches complex and controversial subjects with simplicity and he invariably makes clear what his contentions are about. His polished style has been cultivated by a surprisingly long, sustained and productive practice as editor of the well-known journal *Laissez-Faire*.

On Eponymy in Economics and Other Essays is a collection of fourteen papers, grouped into four parts and an appendix. The papers are a fair sample of some of Professor Cole's preferred topics of inquiry, as well as an illustration of the high quality that his scholarly research has achieved. All of these writings, with the exception of the very last one, have already appeared in several accredited journals. Interested readers, including myself, will be grateful to have them together in a single volume.[2]

"On Eponymy in Economics," the title essay for the collection and the sole piece of writing of the first part, is a remarkable review of *An Eponymous Dictionary of Economics*, a very rare and perhaps unique publication of its kind.[3] Cole maintains that this reference book is not only the first *Eponymous Dictionary of Economics*, as the editors assert, but also "the first endeavor of this kind in *any* discipline" (p. 6). Quoting Merton's *Sociology of Science*, Cole points out that "eponymy" is the term

---

[2]Julio Cole has already published two other volumes of essays in Spanish: *La metodología del análisis económico y otros ensayos* (Madrid: Unión Editorial, 2004) and *Cinco pensadores liberales* (Madrid: Unión Editorial, 2016).

[3]Julio Segura and Carlos Rodríguez Braun, *An Eponymous Dictionary of Economics: A Guide to Laws and Theorems Named after Economists* (Cheltenham, UK: Edward Elgar, 2004).

used for the common practice of "affixing the name of the scientist to all or part of what he has found" (p. 3), and then notes that what determines the prevalence of an eponym through time is common usage in scholarly communication, regardless of historical accuracy. He also notes that the eponymic expressions for commonly used scientific concepts will sooner or later tend to become dissociated from the persons they are named for, which leads to the curious result that, with time, though the concept is widely known and understood, all too often little is known about the person it is named for. As he puts it, "it is the concept that is remembered, not the person" (p. 4).

Julio Cole is an excellent reviewer. Besides informing with accuracy about the content of the material reviewed, he adds facts, analysis and ideas that he pieces together in an interesting and enriching way. In so doing, he shows himself to be a scholar of vast and careful readings. His criticisms to the work of others are always made in a respectful tone (they are never defamatory) and with the sincere aims of clarification or supplementation. His pertinent observations often include caveats that relativize his own arguments. When he finds something valuable, he does not hesitate in giving full credit to the author. In spite of the fact that he identifies thirty omissions in the *Eponymous Dictionary*, his judgment is generous: according to him, the *Dictionary*, containing comprehensive descriptions for more than three hundred eponymous terms regularly used in economics, is "a fine work of scholarship and a major contribution to the literature of economics" (p. 12).

The second part of the book ("The Case for Economic Freedom") is composed of three articles. The first one is a strong criticism of the strategy of industrialization based on import substitution, which was formulated by the Economic Commission for Latin America (ECLA/CEPAL) under the leadership of the legendary Raúl Prebisch in the late 1940s. Cole does not find solid empirical support for the hypothesis of a secular decline in the terms of trade of Latin American countries, the main justification for the import substitution strategy. As for the actual results, he notes that interventionist policies for promoting industrialization generated market distortions that caused inefficient allocation of scarce resources and worsened many of the problems that the strategy was supposed to alleviate: external vulnerability increased, inflationary pressures strengthened, and economic growth was insufficient to relieve both unemployment and poverty.

Cole's critique was published in the middle of the "lost decade", when interventionist policies were in retreat and free market approaches were gaining increasing acceptance not only in Latin America but also around the world. The current resurgence of protectionism in some developed countries is intriguing: the United Kingdom has decided to leave the European Union, and Donald Trump won the US presidency with a protectionist discourse. It could be, as Douglas Irwin suggests, that free trade is at risk anew.[4]

The remaining two essays of the second part are suggestions for improving the specifications and clarifying the meaning of econometric models that estimate the contribution of economic freedom to economic growth. These essays are a sample of the author's mastery of econometric techniques. He feels just as comfortable in discussing complex philosophical issues as in dealing with highly technical econometric procedures.

In the third part of the volume ("The Uneasy Case for Patents and Copyrights"), consisting of an essay and a book review, Cole addresses the controversial and increasingly important issue of patents and copyrights in policy discussions. In this carefully drafted essay, originally published in 2001, after a rigorous analysis of the subject, illustrated by representative examples of specific industries and details about the way the regulatory system works, he pronounces himself for opposing "current efforts to broaden the scope of patent and copyright laws" (p. 83). According to him, there is no clear evidence that the benefits of strengthening patents and copyright regulations and enforcing mechanisms surpass the costs.[5]

Cole revisited this subject by means of a book review published in 2011. The author of the referred book, focusing on the administrative procedures of patent offices and their main clients, detects crucial weaknesses in the global patent system that reinforce Cole's tenets. This time, Cole's tone is more assertive. He believes—contrary to what the author of the book suggests—that "today's patent system is ... broken beyond repair" and he goes as far as to formulate a challenging question: "Since the costs are obvious and the benefits doubtful at best, why not just do away with patents altogether?" (p. 93). Cole's interpretation is consistent with a long liberal tradition that emphasizes the costs and

---

[4]See, for example, Douglas A. Irwin, "Free Trade at Risk? An Historical Perspective," International Finance Discussion Papers No. 391 (Federal Reserve System, Dec 1990), and Douglas A. Irwin, *Free Trade under Fire*, 4th ed. (Princeton, NJ: Princeton University Press, 2015).

[5]He points out that, while patents are temporal monopolies granted by law ("a social bad"), there is no strong evidence that patents significantly stimulate invention ("a social good").

distortions that monopolies granted by law generate in the market economy. For him, patents and copyrights are not compatible with the principles of a free society.

The fourth part ("Studies on Milton Friedman") consists of an obituary, an essay on Friedman's ideas about income inequality, and a review of a biography that focuses on Friedman's intellectual life. The obituary is a sincere and very well achieved tribute by a genuine disciple to his inspiring and appreciated mentor. Besides the systematic and didactic presentation of Friedman's main theoretical contributions to economics, Cole narrates some of the fond recollections he has of Friedman as a human being. He recalls that as a young economist residing in Bolivia he maintained a correspondence with the Nobel laureate. Later on, he spent a whole day talking with Professor Friedman at Stanford University, including an invitation to the Faculty Club, where none other than Professor George Stigler joined them for lunch. Summing up this experience, Cole, charged with sincere emotion, writes: "It meant the world to me" (p. 111). This piece of writing is really a model in its genre.

In his essay on Friedman's views about income inequality, Cole shows that, unexpectedly, Friedman—a libertarian by any reasonable definition—was in favor of government intervention in alleviating poverty by means of the "negative income tax." Although hard-core libertarians regard this particular proposal as inconsistent with his more general views on the free market economy, Cole suggests that Friedman's attitude was grounded in compassionate feelings, not in egalitarianism. If that were the case, Cole proclaims, "I like him the better for it" (p. 131).

Cole's review of the book on Friedman's intellectual life is, as always, interesting and well written. Among other things, he highlights the surprising facts, mentioned in the book under review, that Milton Friedman, as a young man, would have praised President Roosevelt's New Deal, and would have even endorsed some Keynesian ideas. In any case, he points out that the circumstances of Friedman's conversion into economic liberalism are still not well established, and probably never will be (p. 134). Cole certainly ranks among the most knowledgeable scholars of Friedman's scientific ideas in the world.

The last part of the book is an appendix of shorter writings that ratifies that Julio Cole is particularly gifted in writing book reviews, very generous in composing forewords and obituaries, and highly creative and rigorous in drafting academic comments.

Julio told me the other day that in rereading these writings for editing this book he experienced a rewarding sensation: he realized that now he liked them even more than when he actually wrote them. Curiously, I had much of the same feeling in reading this appealing collection of papers anew in order to write this foreword. Revisiting good writings is always revealing and suggestive, and I am sure that the readers of this volume will also fully appreciate and enjoy Julio Cole's remarkable talents as a scholar and as a writer.

Gustavo A. Prado Robles
Professor Emeritus
Universidad Autónoma "Gabriel René Moreno"
Santa Cruz de la Sierra, Bolivia
August, 2017

I. EPONYMY IN ECONOMICS

1

ON EPONYMY IN ECONOMICS

> *A great many highly creative scientists ... take it quite for granted, though they are usually too polite or too ashamed to say so, that an interest in the history of science is a sign of failing or unawaken powers* (Medawar, 1996, p. 98).

> *It takes an economist to read an economist* (Stigler, 1982, p. 108).

Though most economists are probably not familiar with the word "eponymy," the concept it relates to is a common and well-known practice, namely, that of "affixing the name of the scientist to all or part of what he has found" (Merton, 1973, p. 298). To be sure, other disciplines are much more eponymy-prone than ours. Medicine, for instance—where practically every organ, disease or procedure becomes routinely attached to someone's name—seems positively addicted to the practice. Mathematicians, for their part, have turned it into an art-form (which is easily verified by examining the table of contents of any recent mathematics journal[1]).

Eponymy, of course, is not limited to scientific and scholarly activity, but is a common feature of everyday language—and a very ancient one too, as attested by the many rivers, towns and cities, even countries, named after persons (real or mythical). In the case of place-names, the role of eponymy is somewhat akin to that in science, since the original intention

---

Published originally in *Independent Review*, 11 (1) (2006): 121-31.

[1]In *Annals of Mathematics*, for instance, the titles of most papers carry at least one (and often two or three) eponymic expressions—and if the title does not, the abstract almost surely will. A typical example: "Feigenbaum-Coullet-Tresser Universality and Milnor's Hairiness Conjecture" (Lyubich, 1999). I swear that I am not making this up.

is usually honorific. In most cases, however, eponymy in everyday life serves an essentially practical purpose, which is to provide a convenient short-hand expression, allowing us to refer to objects or actions that would otherwise require cumbersome description or tedious repetition. Though the eponymic expression may have originated with an honorific intention, through frequent and casual use this original intent often fades from memory, and the expression stays in use while its users remain ignorant (and unconcerned) about who its eponym might be. Nor does this matter much, since for practical purposes an effective eponymic expression only requires that most people know what it means, regardless of whether they know who it was named for. That Bolivia is named after Simón Bolívar is one of those things that are "nice to know," but who *needs* that information? And who knows if "Tom Collins" really existed? Who cares? ("Bloody Mary" was a real person, but how many people know that, and does it matter?)

In economics, the "Laspeyres price index" is a good example of this phenomenon. According to Schumpeter, "a student can no more go through any complete training in economics without hearing of Laspeyres than he can without hearing of A. Smith" (Schumpeter, 1954, p. 1093n). This is true, but also a bit misleading. Any decent economist *must* know who Adam Smith was, whereas very few economists nowadays know anything at all about Etienne Laspeyres (1834–1913), other than the fact that there is a widely used index number formula that happens to carry his name. For better or worse, Laspeyres now belongs to the "Tom Collins" class of eponyms. It is the concept that is remembered, not the person.

In science, though the honorific purpose for eponymy plays a much larger role, the practical purpose is exactly analogous to that in everyday life. As Merton (1973) puts it: "Eponymy [in science] is thus at once a mnemonic and a commemorative device" (p. 273). Moreover, these two purposes need not be compatible, and in fact they may often conflict. Since the practical purpose of eponymy is to efficiently communicate ideas, useful eponymy requires only that the eponymic expression have a commonly accepted meaning. This is true in everyday life, and it is true in science as well. The potential conflict between "practical" and "honorific" eponymy arises from the fact that the former requires only general agreement on what concept corresponds to any given eponymic expression, whereas the latter requires, in addition, historical accuracy: ideally, we should want each concept to be eponymically related to its "true" originator, creator or discoverer. Unfortunately, although strict "eponymic justice" is much to be desired (for its own sake, if for nothing else), we have it on good authority that such an aspiration is in fact a *chimera*. According to Stigler's Law of Eponymy, "no scientific discovery is named after its original discoverer" (Stigler, 1999, p. 277). Though one might question the empirical basis for this depressing proposition (surely it cannot always be *literally* true), it does appear to have *some* basis in fact. Sadly, it is indeed the case that practical eponymy all too often departs, unfairly, from historical accuracy.[2, 3]

Nor is it altogether clear what, if anything, should be done about it. Though the wounded pride of frustrated potential eponyms is not to be taken lightly (especially if/when they are still living), in the grand scheme of things not much damage is done by eponymic inaccuracy, as long as the practical function of eponymy is not impaired. Again, the Laspeyres index is a perfect example. This is a well-defined concept, now and forever linked by common usage to the name of Etienne Laspeyres, and that is that. Whether this gentleman was actually the "true" inventor of this concept is a moot question of no consequence. Indeed, even if it happened to be the case that this concept was really invented by someone else, at this point to start calling it by the name of its "true" inventor would be a pedantic exercise in futility, and anyone who stubbornly insisted on doing so would be considered silly (if not insane). Through time, the eponym that becomes attached to any given scientific concept will be determined by common usage in actual scholarly communication, regardless of historical accuracy, and whether we like it or not.[4]

What *can* impair the practical usefulness of eponymy in science is the sheer proliferation of eponymic expressions. If the practical purpose of

---

[2][Stephen] Stigler's Law of Eponymy (an interesting case of *auto-eponymy*), is at least partly based on an observation made by his father: "If we should ever encounter a case where a theory is named for the correct man, it will be noted" (Stigler, 1966, p. 77). With a discreet (if uncharacteristic) bow to "political correctness," Stigler later quietly changed this to "correct *person*" in the 4th edition (1987, p. 69). Such are the times we live in!

[3]Preferably, "Stigler's Law of Eponymy" should be cited in full, since otherwise it is apt to be confused with two other extant "Stigler's laws": (1) "Stigler's Law of Elasticities," a tongue-in-cheek proposition concerning estimated price-elasticities, formulated by Stigler *père* (Stigler, 1986), and (2) a numerical regularity in the statistical distribution of first digits, also due to Stigler *père* and first reported by Raimi (1976).

[4]This sounds callous (and it is), but need we be reminded of "Keynes's dictum" (which, incidentally, is not included in the book under review)? In the long-run we *are* all dead, and the sad and sorry fact is that history cares little for ruffled feathers or hurt feelings.

eponymy is to facilitate communication, via the coining of mnemonic expressions, then obviously this communication device will be less efficient, the smaller the number of people who know what any given expression means. (A "mnemonic," if I may be pardoned a tautology, is only useful when we actually *remember* what it means.) This is what happens, however, when the number of eponymic expressions "out there" grows beyond a certain point.

Which brings us, finally, to the subject of this review. Though, as mentioned before, economists are still rank amateurs as compared to more eponymically sophisticated disciplines, such as medicine and mathematics, we have nonetheless contributed our fair share to the world's stock of scientific concepts, and we haven't been shy about labeling many of them eponymously either. The proof is this wonderful book,[5] which provides detailed definitions and explanations for more than 300 eponymic expressions commonly used in economics (surely more than enough to tax anyone's memory).

Some of the expressions included in this volume are so well-known and so much a part of the average economist's working vocabulary that they hardly require explanation. Most, however, pertain to their respective sub-fields and therefore are much less likely to be widely known, hence the usefulness of a book such as this.[6] The articles—written by 234 contributors—are of uniformly high quality, and laid out according to a well-conceived editorial format. All of the articles conveniently include references to the relevant literature (often to the papers or books where the respective concepts were originally introduced), and most are helpfully cross-referenced to other related articles.

---

[5] *An Eponymous Dictionary of Economics: A Guide to Laws and Theorems Named after Economists*, edited by Julio Segura and Carlos Rodríguez Braun. Cheltenham, UK and Northampton, MA: Edward Elgar, 2004, xxviii + 280 pp. $150.00. Hardcover. [Hereinafter referred to as S-R.]

[6] Though the editors claim in their Preface that this is the first *Eponymous Dictionary of Economics*, they are actually too modest. As far as I can tell this is the first endeavor of its kind in *any* discipline. Indeed, a fairly diligent search in the Library of Congress catalogue yielded only one book that even remotely resembles this one (Speert, 1958), and it is not a dictionary, but a collection of essays on medical eponymy (see also Brunschwig, 1959). A new, expanded edition of Speert's book was published in 1996, but without the subtitle (Speert, 1996). A *dictionary* of medical eponymy is surely a hopeless task—and nowadays an unnecessary one as well, given the incredibly large and efficient medical indexes and databases available online.

One benefit from having all these expressions collected in one place is the opportunity it provides for investigating certain general questions relating to economic eponymy. What, for instance, are the eponymic propensities of economists regarding the technical designations (*theorem*, *hypothesis*, *law*, etc.) we attach to people's names when coining eponymic expressions? By my count, the most popular term is *theorem* (33 entries), closely followed by *model* (29 entries) and—the hardy perennial of any self-respecting science—*law* (23 entries). Lagging somewhat behind, at 15 entries each, are *effect* and *test* (the latter drawn mostly from our sister science of statistics). Given our penchant for drawing *curves*, I was surprised by this term's poor showing (only 7 entries). A rather flattering composite picture of our discipline emerges from a closer inspection of the frequencies for some other terms: economists tend to be people of *paradox* (12 entries), true enough, but we are also people of *principle* (10 entries), and not much given to *dogma* (only one entry, "Montaigne's"), nor to *vice* and *schemes* (one each, "Ricardian" and "Ponzi", respectively). Economists, mercifully, have no use at all for *deconstruction*, though the frequency of *decomposition* is disquieting (three entries, to which a fourth might have been added: "Cholesky's"). Many of the terms we use are common in other sciences, and thus we have the full panoply of sundry *methods*, *lemmas*, *criteria*, *coefficients*, *mechanisms*, *problems*, *rules*, *hypotheses*, *procedures*, *conditions*, *processes*. Others terms, such as *box* ("Edgeworth's"), are perhaps peculiar to our own subject. At first glance, one item seems to have been mistakenly drawn from medical terminology ("Baumol's disease"[7]). Some items are a little puzzling ("Schumpeter's vision"? "Senior's last hour"?). Others are just plain odd ("Hume's *fork*"?).

The word *dictum* is associated with a special class of eponymic expressions that are not infrequent in economics, and I was rather disappointed to find that in this book they appear hardly at all. In fact, there is only one such item, "Kelvin's dictum," and he wasn't even an economist. (On the other hand, there are so many good candidates for inclusion under this rubric that the resulting dictionary might have ended up as just another book of quotations.) Another type of eponymic expression alludes to famous *debates* in economics (as in the "Keynes-Ohlin debate," the "Lester-Machlup debate," the "Koopmans-Vining debate" and so forth). There are no items of this type in this dictionary, and it would have been useful to include a few (though economists being a contentious breed, a full listing might have required a volume of its own).

---

[7]A better label for this item would have been "Baumol's cost disease."

Though the dictionary is ostensibly devoted to eponymic expressions that denote scientific concepts (as the subtitle implies), in practice the editors interpret their subject a little more broadly than this, which explains the inclusion of two items that would otherwise seem out of place: "Cowles Commission" and "Palgrave's dictionaries."[8] Two other items that might have been included under this broader interpretation of economic eponymy are "Bonar's catalogue," which would have been welcomed by Smithian scholars with an antiquarian bent (though it might have mystified some of our econometric brethren), and the "Summers-Heston database" (Summers and Heston, 1991), which had a tremendous impact on applied work, and literally transformed the study of economic growth in recent decades.

In the Preface, the editors write that "we fancy that we have listed most of the economic eponyms, and also some non-economic, albeit used in our profession .... We hope that the reader will spot few mistakes in the opposite sense; that is, the exclusion of important and widely used eponyms" (p. xxvii). Spurred by this challenge, I racked my brain for several days trying to think of important items they might have missed. I must confess that I was not very successful, and they actually *do* seem to have listed most of the eponymic expressions used in our profession. (I like to think this reflects the editors' thoroughness, rather than my own ignorance and parochialism.[9]) I did come up with a few, though, which I hereby humbly submit:

Friedman test — A statistical test proposed by Milton Friedman to facilitate the analysis of variance under certain conditions (Friedman, 1937). It has become so standard in the field of non-parametric statistics that it is often referred to as simply the "Friedman test," without further

---

[8]Economic lexicography is an interesting subject in its own right, and from this point of view I think it is fair to say that the Segura-Rodríguez dictionary is actually much more "Palgravian" in style than the so-called *New Palgrave* (Eatwell, Milgate and Newman, 1987), which keeps the *name* of the old *Palgrave's Dictionary* (Higgs, 1923-26) but is really an encyclopedia in the style of the *International Encyclopedia of the Social Sciences* (Sills, 1968).

[9]As economists we all know of course that the only really effective way to find out how many important items were left out is to set up a formal contest, with monetary rewards for submissions. There are hordes of clever and cash-starved graduate students out there, and given the proper incentives they would finish the job in no time. The trick is to find a suitably deep-pocketed benefactor willing to fork out the money.

attribution, and thus most of the people who use it routinely are probably not aware that the creator of this useful test and the world-famous economist are in fact the same person.[10] Though it is not much used by economists, it certainly belongs to the category of "laws and theorems named after economists."

F-Twist — A term coined by Samuelson (1963; see also Wong, 1973) to describe one aspect of Milton Friedman's "methodology of positive economics." The "F" of course is for "Friedman," which is interesting because it is a case of what we might call *abbreviated eponymy*. The only other case I can think of that is relevant to our subject is the "F distribution" (discussed in S-R under "Snedecor's F distribution"), named in honor of R. A. Fisher.[11]

Mill's Methods of Induction — This is a surprising omission. Though they are not strictly economic concepts, they are nonetheless very well known—see, for instance, Mackie (1967)—and John Stuart Mill, whatever else he may have been, was definitely an economist. Even more surprising, however, is that in this book there are no entries under Mill at all. It's not as if he were an unoriginal thinker. Stigler (*père*) famously defended Mill's originality in economics against claims to the contrary (Stigler, 1965, pp. 6-11), and though it is true that not every original idea in economics ends up with an eponym attached to it, surely there must be *something* to honor the great man with? Perhaps the "Mill-Marshall condition"?

Inada conditions — This too is a surprising omission, given that they are actually mentioned (*cum* eponym) in the article on "Solow's growth model and residual."[12] An additional dividend from including this item would be

---

[10]See, for instance, Gibbons (1976), pp. 310-17 and Kanji (1999), p. 113. The Friedman test is therefore becoming yet another instance of what, for lack of a better term, I propose to call the "Tom Collins effect": The eponymic expressions for commonly used scientific concepts will, in time, tend to become dissociated from the persons they are named for. This particular case is all the more remarkable because the Friedman test is not, historically speaking, a very old concept. An even more recent example is the "Ellsberg (1961) paradox" (included in S-R). Probably not many people are aware that this concept was proposed by the same Daniel Ellsberg of "Pentagon Papers" fame (Ellsberg, 1972).

[11]In his own work Fisher himself always referred to this concept as the "variance ratio"—see, for instance, Fisher and Yates (1949), p. 35 *et seq.*

[12]Note that the title for this article refers to two different concepts, which should

to double the number of entries under the letter "I" (the only one now being "Itô's lemma").

Sturges' rule — A practical rule proposed by Sturges (1926) for the construction of histograms, learned (and usually quickly forgotten) by every student of Introductory Statistics, often erroneously identified as "Sturge's rule."[13]

Goldfeld-Quandt test — I am of two minds about this one. At one time it was very well-known, since it was the best available test for heteroskedasticity in linear regressions. On the other hand, it was a tedious, time-consuming procedure, and it has been completely supplanted in applied work by the "White test" (included in S-R), which is much easier to use (especially since it was incorporated into the well-known E-Views software package). To paraphrase General Douglas MacArthur, perhaps outdated ideas and concepts should be allowed to simply fade away.

Tobit model — This is an item of considerable eponymic interest, for several reasons:

1. For one thing, it is an example of a special kind of eponymic expression in which the eponym's name (James Tobin in this case) is actually *incorporated* into the technical word for the concept itself. In fact, this may be the reason it was overlooked, since at first glance it doesn't even look like an eponymic expression. This type of eponymy is rare in economics, though quite common in other fields ("watt" and "volt" being prime examples).

2. It is not often that we can pinpoint the exact moment in which a particular eponymic expression was introduced. Since auto-eponymy is rare, eponymic expressions tend to arise through common usage in

---

have been discussed separately: "Solow growth model" and "Solow residual."

[13]That this error is quite common can be verified by a quick Google search. Sloppy and careless scholarship can of course be very irritating, but note that in this case it does not have any practical consequence for the expression's effectiveness as a communication device. This particular mistake is understandable given that the two versions are homophonous, though I also think it is at least partly due to the "Tom Collins effect": Appearances to the contrary (and with apologies to Mr. Sturges), the typical user of this expression does not really care if the correct name is "Sturge" or "Sturges" because the reference is not to the person, but to the concept.

a more or less Hayekian "spontaneous order" process (not included in S-R). Some will "stick" and others not, but in either case the expressions usually arise long after the introduction of the actual scientific concepts they refer to, and we become aware of a common expression only after it has already gained currency, so it is hard to identify the original eponymist. In this case, however, we know exactly when the expression "tobit model" was introduced, and who the eponymist was: "An alternative one-step procedure is the extension of probit analysis developed by Tobin (1958) that we designate the *Tobit model*" (Goldberger, 1964, p. 253).

3.   Finally, though *tobit* is of course a play on *probit* and *logit*, two related (and non-eponymous) concepts, it *might* also be a case of still another type of eponymy, rare in economics but common in other fields and in everyday language: *fictional eponyms* (as in "Oedipus complex," "Pandora's box," etc.). It so happens that in Herman Wouk's novel *The Caine Mutiny* a "midshipman Tobit" makes a brief appearance (Wouk, 1951, p. 46), and we know that this fictional character is based on none other than James Tobin.[14]

A few additional items come to mind, but since space and reader's patience are in short supply, I will simply list them without detailed commentary:

Adam Smith's Impartial Spectator — Smith ([1759] 1976), Coase (1976)

Alchian-Allen theorem — Cowen and Tabarrok (1995)

Böhm-Bawerkian roundaboutness — Böhm-Bawerk ([1921] 1959)

Durbin's h test — Durbin (1970)

Fisher's ideal index — Fisher (1927)

---

[14]We might as well hear it from the eponym himself: "My main claim to fame, a discovery enjoyed by generations of my students, is that, thinly disguised as a midshipman named Tobit, I make a fleeting appearance in Herman Wouk's novel *The Caine Mutiny*. Wouk and I attended the same quick Naval Reserve officers' training school at Columbia in spring 1942, and so did Willy [Keith], the hero of the novel" (Tobin, 2004, p. 102). I don't know if Mr. Tobit appears in the Humphrey Bogart movie as well. Somebody should check this out.

Fisher's consistency tests — Fisher (1927), Ruggles (1967)

Higgs' ratchet effect — Higgs (1987)

Hume's guillotine[15] — Blaug (1992), pp. 112-13

Gwartney-Lawson economic freedom index — Gwartney and Lawson (2003)

Klein-Goldberger model — Adelman and Adelman (1959)

Mincer returns — Rosen (1992)[16], Psacharopoulos (1994)

Nordhaus-Scherer model — Scherer (1972)

Ricardo's point — Takayama (1972), p. 120 *passim*

Studentized range test[17] — Pearson and Stephens (1964)

Sweezy's "kinky demand curve" — Sweezy (1939)

Viner-Wong theorem — Silberberg (1999)

Waaler curves[18] — Fogel (1994)

Some of these are important omissions, others perhaps less so. However, even adding them all up (plus a few others mentioned in passing throughout this essay) does not really amount to more than a minor dent in what is, in my view, a fine work of scholarship and a major contribution

---

[15]For some reason, Hume tends to be associated with very odd eponymic expressions. (Note, in passing, how this one is elegantly constructed by affixing an eponym to *another* eponymic expression.)

[16]The title of Rosen's paper is an intriguing variation on standard eponymic technique.

[17]This expression is (obviously) derived from "Student's t" (included in S-R), which is itself of eponymic interest, because it is a rare case in which the *eponym* is also a *pseudonym*.

[18]This is, strictly speaking, a bio-medical concept, though it has been used very creatively by Robert Fogel to help explain certain patterns in economic history.

to the literature of economics. Its quality speaks for itself, and the best way to close this review is to let it do just that. In describing the Eatwell-Newman-Milgate *New Palgrave*, the author of the article on "Palgrave's dictionaries" writes: "… it is an unquestionably authoritative reference work on economic theory and the work of those economists who contributed to its development" (p. 193). Word for word, the same thing can be said about this volume. Julio Segura and Carlos Rodríguez Braun have done us proud, and they deserve our thanks.

REFERENCES

Adelman, Irma and Frank L. Adelman. 1959. Dynamic Properties of the Klein-Goldberger Model. *Econometrica*, 27 (4): 596-625.

Blaug, Mark. 1992. *The Methodology of Economics, or How Economists Explain*, 2nd ed. Cambridge: Cambridge University Press.

Böhm-Bawerk, Eugen von. [1921] 1959. *Capital and Interest*, 3 vols. George D. Huncke and Hans F. Sennholz, trans. South Holland, Ill.: Libertarian Press.

Brunschwig, Alexander. 1959. Review of *Obstetric and Gynecologic Milestones: Essays in Eponymy* by Harold Speert. *Bulletin of the Medical Library Association*, 47 (3): 357.

Coase, R. H. 1976. Adam Smith's View of Man. *Journal of Law and Economics*, 19 (3): 529-46.

Cowen, Tyler and Alexander Tabarrok. 1995. Good Grapes and Bad Lobsters: Applying the Alchian and Allen Theorem. *Economic Inquiry*, 33 (2): 253-56.

Durbin, James. 1970. Testing for Serial Correlation in Least-Squares Regression When Some of the Regressors are Lagged Dependent Variables. *Econometrica*, 38 (3): 410-21.

Eatwell, John, Murray Milgate and Peter Newman, eds. 1987. *The New Palgrave: A Dictionary of Economics*, 4 vols. London: Macmillan.

Ellsberg, Daniel. 1961. Risk, Ambiguity, and the Savage Axioms. *Quarterly Journal of Economics*, 75 (4): 643-69.

Ellsberg, Daniel. 1972. *Papers on the War*. New York: Simon and Schuster.

Fisher, Irving. 1927. *The Making of Index Numbers: A Study of their Varieties, Tests and Reliability*, 3rd ed. Boston: Houghton Mifflin.

Fisher, Ronald A. and Frank Yates. 1949. *Statistical Tables for Biological, Agricultural and Medical Research*, 3rd ed. London: Oliver and Boyd.

Fogel, Robert W. 1994. Economic Growth, Population Theory, and Physiology: The Bearing of Long-Term Processes on the Making of

Economic Policy. *American Economic Review*, 84 (3): 369-95.

Friedman, Milton. 1937. The Use of Ranks to Avoid the Assumption of Normality Implicit in the Analysis of Variance. *Journal of the American Statistical Association*, 32 (200): 675-701.

Gibbons, Jean Dickinson. 1976. *Nonparametric Methods for Quantitative Analysis*. New York: Holt, Rinehart and Winston.

Goldberger, Arthur S. 1964. *Econometric Theory*. New York: John Wiley & Sons.

Gwartney, James D. and Robert A. Lawson. 2003. The Concept and Measurement of Economic Freedom. *European Journal of Political Economy*, 19 (3): 405-30.

Higgs, Henry, ed. 1923-26. *Palgrave's Dictionary of Political Economy*, 3 vols. London: Macmillan.

Higgs, Robert. 1987. *Crisis and Leviathan: Critical Episodes in the Growth of American Government*. Oxford: Oxford University Press.

Kanji, Gopal K. 1999. *100 Statistical Tests*. London: Sage Publications.

Lyubich, Mikhail. 1999. Feigenbaum-Coullet-Tresser Universality and Milnor's Hairiness Conjecture. *Annals of Mathematics*, 149 (2): 319-420.

Mackie, J. L. 1967. Mill's Methods of Induction. In Paul Edwards (ed.), *Encyclopedia of Philosophy*, vol. 5, pp. 324-32. New York: Macmillan.

Medawar, Peter. 1996. *The Strange Case of the Spotted Mice and Other Classic Essays on Science*. Oxford: Oxford University Press.

Merton, Robert K. 1973. *The Sociology of Science: Theoretical and Empirical Investigations*. Chicago: University of Chicago Press.

Pearson, E. S. and M. A. Stephens. 1964. The Ratio of Range to Standard Deviation in the Same Normal Sample. *Biometrika*, 51 (3/4): 484-87.

Psacharopoulos, George. 1994. Returns to Investment in Education: A Global Update. *World Development*, 22 (9): 1325-43.

Raimi, Ralph A. 1976. The First Digit Problem. *American Mathematical*

Monthly, 83 (7): 521-38.

Rosen, Sherwin. 1992. Mincering Labor Economics. *Journal of Economic Perspectives*, 6 (2): 157-70.

Ruggles, Richard. 1967. Price Indexes and International Price Comparisons. In William Fellner, *et al.*, *Ten Economic Studies in the Tradition of Irving Fisher*, pp. 171-205. New York: John Wiley & Sons.

Samuelson, Paul A. 1963. Problems of Methodology: Discussion. *American Economic Review*, 53 (2): 231-36.

Scherer, F. M. 1972. Nordhaus' Theory of Optimal Patent Life: A Geometric Reinterpretation. *American Economic Review*, 62 (3): 422-27.

Schumpeter, Joseph A. 1954. *History of Economic Analysis*. London: George Allen & Unwin.

Silberberg, Eugene. 1999. The Viner-Wong Envelope Theorem. *Journal of Economic Education*, 30 (1): 75-79.

Sills, David L., ed. 1968. *International Encyclopedia of the Social Sciences*, 17 vols. New York: Macmillan.

Smith, Adam. [1759] 1976. *The Theory of Moral Sentiments*. A. L. Macfie and D. D. Raphael, eds. Oxford: Oxford University Press.

Speert, Harold. 1958. *Obstetric and Gynecologic Milestones: Essays in Eponymy*. New York: Macmillan.

Speert, Harold. 1996. *Obstetric and Gynecologic Milestones*. New York: Parthenon Publishing Group.

Stigler, George J. 1965. *Essays in the History of Economics*. Chicago: University of Chicago Press.

Stigler, George J. 1966. *The Theory of Price*, 3rd ed. New York: Macmillan.

Stigler, George J. 1982. *The Economist as Preacher and Other Essays*. Chicago: University of Chicago Press.

Stigler, George J. 1986. Stigler's Law of Demand and Supply Elasticities.

In Kurt Leube (ed)., *The Essence of Stigler*, pp. 361-67. Stanford, CA: Hoover Institution Press.

Stigler, George J. 1987. *The Theory of Price*, 4th ed. New York: Macmillan.

Stigler, Stephen M. 1999. *Statistics on the Table*. Cambridge, MA: Harvard University Press.

Sturges, Herbert A. 1926. The Choice of a Class Interval. *Journal of the American Statistical Association*, 21 (153): 65-66.

Summers, Robert and Alan Heston. 1991. The Penn World Table (Mark 5): An Expanded Set of International Comparisons, 1950-1988. *Quarterly Journal of Economics*, 106 (2): 327-68.

Sweezy, Paul M. 1939. Demand under Conditions of Oligopoly. *Journal of Political Economy*, 47 (4): 568-73.

Takayama, Akira. 1972. *International Trade*. New York: Holt, Rinehart and Winston.

Tobin, James. 1958. Estimation of Relationships for Limited Dependent Variables. *Econometrica*, 26 (1): 24-36.

Tobin, James. 2004. James Tobin. In William Breit and Barry T. Hirsch (eds.), *Lives of the Laureates: Eighteen Nobel Economists*, 4th ed., pp. 95-113. Cambridge, MA: MIT Press.

Wong, Stanley. 1973. The "F-Twist" and the Methodology of Paul Samuelson. *American Economic Review*, 63 (3): 312-25.

Wouk, Herman. 1951. *The Caine Mutiny*. New York: Doubleday & Co.

II. The Case for Economic Freedom

2

THE FALSE PROMISE OF
PROTECTIONISM FOR LATIN AMERICA

Economics, "as every schoolboy knows," is concerned with the efficient use of scarce resources, and particularly with determining the institutional framework which is most likely to result in an "efficient" outcome as judged by certain specific criteria. Adam Smith found such a framework in his "obvious and simple system of natural liberty," wherein each individual, by maximizing his own welfare, is at the same time led as if by "an invisible hand to promote an end which was no part of his intention." Indeed, as Smith observed, "by pursuing his own interest he frequently promotes that of the society more effectually than when he really intends to promote it."[1] In the international sphere the corollary to Smith's "obvious and simple system" is of course free and open international trade.

On the other hand, underlying much of modern theorizing on economic development is the view that the classical case for free trade cannot be realistically applied to the less developed countries (LDCs) because of its alleged highly restrictive, if implicit, technological and institutional assumptions, and because it is based on a *static* theory of the allocation of *given* resources and hence irrelevant in the essentially dynamic context of the problems posed by economic growth. Based on the obvious observation that the LDCs are indeed quite different from the advanced countries, not only in absolute levels of material welfare but also in social attitudes and institutional settings, the idea quite naturally arose

Published originally in *Journal of Economic Growth*, 1 (4) (1986): 28-37.

[1]Adam Smith, *An Inquiry into the Nature and Causes of the Wealth of Nations*, Cannan edition (New York: Random House, 1937), pp. 423, 651.

that nothing short of a new "unorthodox" economics would do. In contrast to the "orthodox" or "classical" theory, the "new" economics was generally skeptical regarding the allocational efficiency of the price system in the LDCs, and instead sought to justify direct government intervention to promote economic growth by supplanting the free market price mechanism.

However, whatever "the limitations of the special case" may have been,[2] most of the assumptions of the new economics were, in turn, demonstrably false. Indeed, a careful examination of the data shows that the new theories never had any factual basis, though they were never lacking in the intuitive and emotional plausibility which explains their widespread acceptance. More importantly, the *policies* which have been justified by the new economics have arguably resulted in an aggravation of the very problems which they were intended to alleviate. In no instance is this quite so evident as in the case of the protectionist policy of import-substituting industrialization on which the Latin American countries embarked upon after World War II, largely inspired by the theories of Raúl Prebisch.

The Prebisch Thesis and its Background

The theoretical case for protected, import-substituting industriali-zation in Latin America was based first and foremost on a pessimistic view of the long-run development prospects of LDCs under a regime of free international trade. This view stemmed from an alleged secular decline in the terms of trade of these countries, identified, by and large, as exporters of primary raw materials, *vis-à-vis* the exports of manufactured products of developed, industrialized economies.

Clearly, this departed radically from the liberal view derived from the classical theory of international trade, which has always emphasized the gains accruing to both parties engaged in free trade, and the benefits derived from the international division of labor. In the new economics, however, the international economic order was regarded, not as the outcome of an efficient process of resource allocation and specialization according to comparative costs and relative factor endowments—the working of Adam Smith's "invisible hand" on a global scale—but rather

---

[2]To quote the title of the influential article by Dudley Seers, "The Limitations of the Special Case," *Bulletin of the Oxford Institute of Economics and Statistics*, 25 (May 1963): 77-98.

as the end result of centuries of colonial exploitation which still exhibits the marks of neo-colonial "dependence."

To be sure, theories of colonial and neo-imperialistic exploitation are anything but new, though the emphasis on the terms of trade is of relatively recent origin, and can be traced to the publication, in 1949, of a United Nations report entitled "Post-War Price Relations in Trade between Under-developed and Industrialized Countries."[3] The main findings of that study, which seem to indicate a sharp deterioration in the terms of trade of primary products in relation to manufactures over the period 1876 to 1938, are presented in Table 1 (page 31). (It is not always sufficiently stressed that, due to data limitations at the time of the original report, this series is actually the reciprocal of the terms of trade of the United Kingdom, and the conclusion as to the movement in the terms of trade of primary producing countries is valid only to the extent that prices of British imports [mainly primary products] and exports [manufactures] are, in fact, representative of world trends in primary and manufactured products, respectively.)

These data were used by Dr. Raúl Prebisch as the basis of his influential report on "The Economic Development of Latin America and its Principal Problems,"[4] which presented his explanation of the observed deterioration, and his theory of the secular *tendency* towards deterioration of primary terms of trade. Although his main interest was in the problems of Latin America, his generalizations are applicable to all primary producing countries (the world's "periphery" in his terminology).

In Latin America, Prebisch held, "reality is undermining the outdated schema of the international division of labor .... " Conventional international trade theories were outdated as well, he argued. Prebisch summarized the conventional wisdom thusly:

It is true that the reasoning on the economic advantages of the inter-

---

[3]United Nations, "Post-War Price Relations in Trade between Under-developed and Industrialized Countries," Document E/CN. I/Sub.3/W.5 (New York, Feb 1949).

[4]"The Economic Development of Latin America and its Principal Problems" (New York, United Nations, 1950). This report was published originally without attribution, and later reprinted under Prebisch's name in *Economic Bulletin for Latin America*, 7 (Feb 1962): 1-22, and in G. M. Meier (ed.), *Leading Issues in Development Economics* (New York: Oxford University Press, 1964), pp. 339-43, from which the following citations are quoted.

national division of labour is theoretically sound, but it is usually forgotten that it is based upon an assumption which has been conclusively proved false by facts. According to this assumption, the benefits of technical progress tend to be distributed alike over the whole community, either by the lowering of prices or the corresponding raising of incomes. The countries producing raw materials obtain their share of these benefits through international exchange, and therefore have no need to industrialize. If they were to do so, their lesser efficiency would result in their losing the conventional advantages of such exchange.[5]

According to Prebisch, however,

> If, ..., the concept of the community is extended to include the periphery of the world economy, a serious error is implicit in the generalization. The enormous benefits that derive from increased productivity have not reached the periphery in a measure comparable to that obtained by the peoples of the great industrial countries.[6]

Though he presents no supporting evidence, Prebisch states that "technical progress seems to have been greater in industry than in the primary production of peripheral countries ...." Given this assumption, then,

> ... if prices had been reduced in proportion to increasing productivity, the reduction should have been less in the case of primary products than in that of manufactures, so that as the disparity between productivities increased, the price relationship between the two should have shown a steady improvement in favor of the countries of the periphery.[7]

Appealing to the data in Table 1, Prebisch argues that the actual development of the terms of trade had been the exact opposite:

> ... the price relation turned steadily against primary production from the 1870's until the Second World War .... With the same amount of primary products, only 63 per cent of the finished manufactures which could be bought in the 1860's were to be had in the 1930's; in other words, an average of 58.6 per cent more primary products was needed to buy the same amount of finished manufactures. The price relation, therefore, moved against the periphery, contrary to what should have happened had

---

[5]*Ibid.*, p. 339.

[6]*Ibid.*, p. 340.

[7]*Ibid.*

prices fallen as costs decreased as a result of higher productivity.[8]

Generalizing from these developments, Prebisch went on to conclude that the net result had been a massive income transfer from the periphery to the centers.[9]

Prebisch's initial explanation of this phenomenon relied on an asymmetrical behavior of wages in the industrial centers during the course of the trade cycle, although in later theoretical work he has attributed the secular decline to differences in the income-elasticities of demand for primary and manufactured products, and in the rates of spread of technological improvements.[10] He takes it for granted that the income-elasticity of demand for primary products is generally lower that the income-elasticity of demand for Latin American imports of industrial products, and that, consequently, "import substitution ... is the only way to correct the effects on peripheral growth of disparities in foreign trade elasticities."[11]

Critics often take issue with this "well-established fact" on the grounds that in the empirical literature the only well-established fact is Engel's law of a less than unitary income-elasticity of demand for *food* products, which certainly does not apply to primary products such as minerals, nor to *all* agricultural products (such as wool, jute, cotton, etc.), and not even to *all* food products. However, it is rather idle to criticize the assumptions of the theory, if even the *fact* that it purports to explain is open to question.

---

[8]*Ibid.*, pp. 340-41.

[9]According to Prebisch, "... while the centres kept the whole benefit of the technical development of their industries, the peripheral countries transferred to them a share of the fruits of their own technical progress" (*ibid.*, p. 342). Similarly, Hans Singer at about the same time argued that under the prevailing scheme the gains of technical progress were distributed to producers as higher incomes, while in primary producing countries these gains accrued to consumers via lower prices. Accordingly, "the industrialized countries have had the best of both worlds, both as consumers of primary commodities and as producers of manufactured articles, whereas the underdeveloped countries have had the worst of both worlds, as consumers of manufactures and as producers of raw materials" (Hans Singer, "The Distribution of Gains between Investing and Borrowing Countries," *American Economic Review*, 40 [May 1950], p. 479).

[10]Raúl Prebisch, "Commercial Policy in the Underdeveloped Countries," *American Economic Review*, 49 (May 1959): 251-73.

[11]*Ibid.*, pp. 252-53.

Certainly, the assumptions of the Prebisch thesis are consistent with a secular decline in primary terms of trade, and in this sense they can be said to "explain" such a phenomenon. An evaluation of the Prebisch thesis, however, requires a prior empirical effort to determine whether the alleged secular decline is a *fact* at all, since explanations of nonexistent facts are redundant, and their theoretical discussion wasted effort, to say the least. These empirical issues will be addressed below, but a prior examination of certain conceptual issues involved in the terms of trade is in order.

Terms of Trade Concepts and Their Interpretation

In most statistical work, and in nearly all public and professional discussion, it is the *commodity* or *net barter* terms of trade that are involved, which are defined as an index of the average price of a country's commodity exports in terms of its commodity imports. Statistically, if $P_x(t)$ is an index of the prices of a country's exports during a certain period t, and $P_m(t)$ is an index of the prices of the country's imports during the same time period, then the index of the commodity terms of trade is defined as $T_c(t) = 100 \times [P_x(t) \div P_m(t)]$, and is a measure of the movement in the country's terms of trade up to period t as compared with the base period of the import and export price indices. Clearly, the index thus defined, like any other price index, can only indicate relative movements, that is, whether in any given period the terms of trade are more or less favorable than in some other period chosen for comparison, and judgments as to whether the terms of trade are favorable (or unfavorable) in some absolute sense are not warranted on the basis of the price indices alone.

Although the commodity terms of trade are often used as an indicator of national welfare, or of changes in the gains from trade, they are actually not a very reliable indicator, and recognition of this fact has resulted in the development of several alternative definitions. To be sure, an *improvement* in the commodity terms of trade can, under most conditions, be associated unambiguously with an increase in the country's welfare, though the converse proposition may not necessarily hold if there has been an increase in the productivity of the export sector. Thus, supposing for a moment that prices are constant, a productivity increase in the export sector will result in a welfare gain since the same amount of factors of production (resources) used to produce the exported good can be exchanged for a larger amount of imported goods, even though the commodity terms of trade have not changed. In general, the country's welfare will decrease only if the decline in the commodity terms of trade more than offsets the increase in productivity, and therefore the relevant terms of trade concept is the *single factoral* terms of trade, defined as $T_{sf}(t) = T_c(t) \times F_x(t)$, where $F_x(t)$ is an index of the change in the productivity of the export sector. Given the theoretical and empirical difficulties involved in choosing and measuring an appropriate index of productivity, the single factoral terms of trade are rarely, if ever, used in statistical analysis, though they should be clearly borne in mind in interpreting observed changes in the commodity terms of trade since, though the latter may be likened to a zero-sum game, it is quite possible for the underlying single factoral terms of trade to improve simultaneously for *both* trading partners.[12]

These conceptual issues thus preclude the drawing of any facile inferences from observed movements in the simple commodity terms of trade. The problems are compounded by the practical difficulties posed by the empirical measurement of the underlying price indices.

The measurement of aggregative price trends over time is always problematic due to shifts in consumption patterns between different classes of goods as a result of substitution in consumption in response to changing relative prices. The kind of price comparisons between very distant time periods required for the determination of long-run terms of trade are further complicated—to the extent of actually losing much of their meaning—as a result of the introduction of new products and of changes in the quality of existing goods. In the specific case of price comparisons for the terms of trade of primary products, the practical difficulty of taking these factors into account introduces a statistical bias into the estimates, as they will have a greater impact upon the index of imported manufactures than upon the export price index, since primary products do not change much in either quality or variety.

Both of these factors tend to bias the measurement of import prices

---

[12]Other definitions include the *double factoral* terms of trade, $T_{df}(t) = T_c(t) \times [F_x(t) \div F_m(t)]$, which takes into account changes in the productivity of the foreign export sector, and purports to measure changes in the terms on which *resources* are exchanged, and the *income* terms of trade, $T_i(t) = T_c(t) \times Q_x(t)$, where $Q_x(t)$ is an index of the *volume* of exports. The double factoral is interesting in certain theoretical contexts, and was in fact the major terms of trade concept in early formulations of classical trade theory, though it is not very relevant from the welfare point of view of an importing country. The income terms of trade, introduced by G. S. Dorrance ("The Income Terms of Trade," *Review of Economic Studies*, 16 [1948-49]: 50-56), is interesting from the point of view of changes in the "capacity to import," but as an indicator of changes in welfare it can be quite unreliable. For a more complete technical discussion of these concepts see M. C. Kemp, "International Trade: Terms of Trade," *International Encyclopedia of the Social Sciences* (1968), vol. 8, pp. 105-08.

paid by primary exporters in an upward direction. Clearly, improvements in quality will tend to overstate the increase in *real* prices to the extent that part of the price change is simply a reflection of better quality. On the other hand, it is reasonably well-established that the price history of a new product is one of rapid decline in its early stages. But since new products by definition are difficult to include in commodity samples of price indices, they are eventually included only upon revisions of the indices, which are then linked to earlier series. The initial exclusion of these products, therefore, tends to underestimate the relative price decline of the total commodity list.

Another upward bias is due to the fact that price indices of international trade are usually not based upon actual prices, but rather upon "implicit unit values." A unit value index differs from a price index in that it measures changes in average values per physical unit, regardless of whether they are due to price changes, or to changes in size, quality or other circumstances. Unit value indices are generally computed from customs data on values and quantities. The unit value for each component series is derived by dividing quantities into values, and the individual unit value series are then collected into an overall index. Unit value series are often unreliable approximations to the underlying price changes since even for relatively simple types of products, such as steel pipe, changes in the mix of products (e.g., from narrow to wide pipe, from thick to thin, etc.) can change the unit values even if not a single price has changed. A major handicap is in the case of complex manufactures such as machinery, where strict quantity data are not collected as the number of units is meaningless when size, design, power and other product characteristics vary widely from one unit to another. In the special case of machinery imports, the unit values are computed simply by dividing the value of imports by their physical weight, and as machinery become more efficient but less bulky—a common form of technical improvement—the unit values will show an increase, even if prices remain unchanged, while the price per efficiency unit may have actually declined.

Given these upward biases in the measurement of changes in prices of imported manufactures, the estimated terms of trade of primary producing (manufactures importing) countries will have a systematic downward bias, i.e., they are biased toward the indication of deteriorating terms of trade, a bias which will, moreover, increase through time. Hence, even a substantial decline in the observed commodity terms of trade may be consistent with the hypothesis of no change in the true commodity terms of trade, and an actual improvement in the single factoral. At his point, one may honestly wonder what purpose may be served by the examination of long term movements of price series which in the best of cases provide useful information only under the assumption that all else is constant.

The Factual Record

As stated previously, the initial Prebisch thesis was based upon the movement in the British commodity terms of trade up to 1938. The biases summarized above explain a large share of the trend in the historical series, but there are some additional considerations which raise doubts as to the adequacy of the British data as a (reciprocal) measure of primary terms of trade. To begin with, and granting the assumption that the terms of trade of industrial countries move inversely to those of primary producers, it is not clear that the British series is representative of industrial countries taken as a group. Complete series for the entire period covered in Table 1 are not available, but Kindleberger has provided estimates of the commodity terms of trade of industrial European countries for the period 1900-52 which suggest that the British data are *not* representative.[13] Though Kindleberger's data do show an improvement in European terms of trade of about 34 % between 1913 and 1938, a movement roughly equal to that of the British series over the same period, the European terms of trade had *declined* 13 % from 1900 to 1913, as opposed to a decline of only 1 % in the British series. Thus the increase in the Kindleberger series over the entire period 1900-38 is less than 19 % (which, it is well to recall, has no adjustment for statistical bias in the price series).

Even conceding the relevance of the oft-cited British series, the behavior of the British terms of trade *prior* to 1876 is clearly relevant in the context of the secular decline hypothesis. Though price data for the remote past are naturally imprecise, the weight of the available evidence suggests that the use of 1876 as a comparison base is somewhat misleading because British terms of trade declined steadily and substantially during the first half of the 19th century, and they appear to have been at their lowest historical levels precisely in the period 1860-80.[14]

---

[13]Charles P. Kindleberger, *The Terms of Trade: A European Case Study* (Cambridge: MIT Press, 1956), Table 2-1, p. 12.

[14]See the two major articles by Albert H. Imlah, "Real Values in British Foreign Trade, 1798-1853," *Journal of Economic History*, 8 (Nov 1948): 133-52, and "Terms of Trade in the United Kingdom, 1798-1913," *Journal of Economic History*, 10 (Nov 1950): 170-94; see also T. S. Ashton, "The Standard of Life of

A final problem in the interpretation of the 1876-1938 British series is posed by transportation costs. The basic British export price index is on a F.O.B. ("free on board") basis, while import prices are measured C.I.F., that is, including transportation charges. Clearly, an improvement in British terms of trade due to less expensive C.I.F. imports resulting from a reduction of shipping costs is no indication of a corresponding decline in foreign terms of trade. In fact, freight rates fell by about 50 % between 1870 and 1913. According to Baldwin's estimates this accounted for about 5 percentage points of the 19 % improvement in British commodity terms of trade over this period.[15] Ellsworth goes so far as to state that from 1876 to 1905 the larger share, perhaps even the *entire* decline in British primary import prices, was due to the sharp decline in freight rates. Moreover, since the prices of British manufactured exports declined by 15 %, the terms of trade of primary producing countries may well have improved over that period, as opposed to the 14 % decline as indicated by Table 1.[16]

The much-touted long run decline in primary terms of trade as of 1938 is therefore at best unproven. Post-war price developments do not support the secular decline hypothesis either. Prebisch glossed over the 7 % improvement in primary terms of trade, as implied by the British series between 1938 and 1947, which he attributed to a minor cyclical movement.[17] In a later influential report[18] he much-emphasized the decline in primary terms of trade during the latter half of the 1950s. Clearly, however, no far-reaching conclusions can be drawn regarding the secular decline hypothesis unless the price trends of the intervening 1948-55 period are considered as well. As it happens, these years witnessed a spec-

---

the Workers in England, 1790-1830," in F. A. Hayek (ed.), *Capitalism and the Historians* (Chicago: University of Chicago Press, 1954), pp. 136-43.

[15]Robert E. Baldwin, "Secular Movements in the Terms of Trade," *American Economic Review*, 45 (May 1955), p. 269.

[16]Paul T. Ellsworth, "The Terms of Trade between Primary Producing and Industrial Countries," *Inter-American Economic Affairs*, 10 (Summer 1956), pp. 55-56.

[17]Prebisch, "The Economic Development of Latin America," p. 341.

[18]Raúl Prebisch, "Los problemas del desarrollo de los países periféricos y los términos de intercambio," in J. Theberge (ed.), *Economía del comercio y desarrollo* (Buenos Aires: Amorrortu, 1968), pp. 331-42. Reprinted from an original report entitled *Towards a Dynamic Development Policy for Latin America* (New York: United Nations, 1963).

Table 1 — Ratio of Prices of Primary Commodities to those of
Manufactured Goods (Average Import and Export Prices)
(1876-80 = 100)

Periods	Amount of finished products obtainable for a given quantity of primary commodities
1876-80	100.0
1881-85	102.4
1886-90	96.3
1891-95	90.1
1896-1900	87.1
1901-05	84.6
1906-10	85.8
1911-13	85.8
...	...
1921-25	67.3
1926-30	73.3
1931-35	62.0
1936-38	64.1
...	...
1946-47	68.7

Source: United Nations, "Post-War Price Relations in Trade between Under-developed and Industrialized Countries," Document E/CN. I/Sub.3/W.5, 23 February 1949.

tacular *rise* in the terms of trade of developing countries, a rise which was far from completely offset by the subsequent decline (see Table 2). From 1937 to 1948 developing countries' terms of trade improved 8 %, and those of Latin America by over 20 %. Developing countries' terms of trade improved a further 52 % by 1951, and though they subsequently declined during the rest of the 1950s, as stressed by Prebisch, by 1959 they were still 23 % above their pre-war levels. (Again, it must be recalled that these estimates have no adjustment for quality changes and other sources of bias.)

For the post-1959 period we rely on the two terms of trade series reported in Table 3: (i) CEPAL's index of Latin American commodity terms of trade, which is a weighted average of the terms of trade of 19 Latin American countries, and (ii) the IMF's price index of the 30 main primary commodities (excluding oil) exported by developing countries, deflated by the unit value index of imported manufactures. From 1959 to 1970 both series show minor fluctuations, but on the whole they were remarkable stable.

If the secular decline hypothesis has any relevance at all, *some* evidence would have had to show up by the 1970s. Indeed, even if there had been no long run change in the real terms of trade, one would have expected a decline in the measured commodity terms of trade due to the statistical biases involved (which would still have been consistent with a significant improvement in the single factoral). The statistical record as of the mid-1970s admits of no clear-cut conclusion in this regard.[19] In the specific case of Latin America, the terms of trade have certainly been quite variable in recent years, but considering that in 1959 they were about 10 % above their 1937 level, the measured Latin American terms of trade did not begin to approach their 1937 level until about 1983.[20] It might be argued, however, that this is partly due to the fact that some Latin American countries are major oil exporters. Indeed, the terms of trade of non-oil exporting Latin American countries deteriorated by about 40 % between 1970 and 1983 and, assuming that non-oil Latin American terms of trade moved proportionally to those of Latin America as a whole prior to 1970, it can be roughly estimated that they were about 30 % below their

---

[19]See G. F. Ray, "The 'Real' Price of Primary Products," *National Institute Economic Review*, 81 (Aug 1977): 72-76, and John Spraos, "The Statistical Debate on the Net Barter Terms of Trade between Primary Commodities and Manufactures," *Economic Journal*, 90 (Mar 1980): 107-28.

[20]It is well to note that in the case of Latin America, comparisons with the 1930s can be greatly affected by the choice of a particular base year, since that region's terms of trade were quite variable at the time:

1930	105	1935	91
1931	82	1936	97
1932	88	1937	100
1933	82	1938	95
1934	94	1939	94

Source: Economic Commission for Latin America (CEPAL), *América Latina: Relación de Precios del Intercambio* (Santiago de Chile: Naciones Unidas, 1976), p. 25. See also D. W. Baerresen *et al.*, *Latin American Trade Patterns* (Washington: Brookings Institution, 1965), Table B, p. 22.

1937 level as of 1983. On the other hand, most of this deterioration has been due to a development that has nothing to do with the Prebisch thesis, namely, the OPEC oil price surge. In fact, the relative price of primary products *vis-à-vis* manufactures, the relevant concept in terms of the Prebisch thesis, shows a deterioration of only 12 % from 1970 to 1983. Furthermore, though primary terms of trade appear to have deteriorated by about 20 % in the period 1959-83, if the data in Table 2 are taken as a proximate measure of primary/manufactures terms of trade prior to 1959, the nominal deterioration of primary terms of trade for the full period 1937-83 has been at most 10 %. (Once more, no great significance can be attached to this statistic in the absence of adjustments for quality change and other courses of bias.)

Ideas Have Consequences

The secular decline hypothesis is thus utterly lacking in factual basis. Even if the Prebisch thesis were true, however, one may well wonder what kind of benefits the LDCs were supposed to derive from protectionism, and whether the actual outcome was consistent with the objectives pursued.

Broadly speaking, the main objectives were twofold. Firstly, and quite apart from forestalling the long-run impact of declining terms of trade, import substitution was seen as a way out of the foreign exchange "bottle-

Table 2 — Terms of Trade (1937 = 100)

	Underdeveloped Countries	Latin America
1937	100	100
1948	108	123
1951	160	138
1954	128	139
1957	127	128
1959	123	110

Sources: (1) Underdeveloped countries: Theodore Morgan, "Relaciones económicas entre las naciones: Esquema del comercio de mercancías," in B. Hoselitz (ed.), *La economía y la idea de humanidad* (México: Herrero, 1967), Table 3, p. 164; (2) Latin America: CEPAL, *América Latina: Relación de precios del intercambio* (Santiago de Chile: Naciones Unidas, 1976), p. 25.

Table 3 — Terms of Trade, 1959-83 (1970 = 100)

| | Latin America | | Primary Products |
	Total	Non-Oil Producing Countries	
1959	102	...	108
1960	102	...	106
1961	100	...	101
1962	94	...	98
1963	95	...	105
1964	97	...	109
1965	93	...	105
1966	95	...	105
1967	93	...	98
1968	95	...	98
1969	96	...	102
1970	100	100	100
1971	97	...	90
1972	100	...	93
1973	113	...	124
1974	131	...	130
1975	114	82	93
1976	119	...	105
1977	126	98	117
1978	113	...	98
1979	117	82	100
1980	121	...	98
1981	110	66	88
1982	101	...	80
1983	94	...	88

Sources: (1) Latin America: CEPAL, *América Latina: Relación de precios del intercambio* (Santiago de Chile: Naciones Unidas, 1976), p. 25, and *Estudio económico de América Latina y el Caribe 1983*, vol. 1 (Santiago de Chile: Naciones Unidas, 1985), pp. 40-41; (2) Primary Products: K.-Y. Chu and T. K. Morrison, "The 1981-82 Recession and Non-Oil Primary Commodity Prices," *IMF Staff Papers*, 31 (March 1984), Table 1, p. 98.

neck" faced by LDCs. According to this argument, a highly income-elastic demand for imports would tend to rise in the course of economic growth, outstripping the capacity to import from export revenues, which need not rise *pari passu* with import demand, and generally would not do so. This placed a binding constraint on the possibilities for growth, which depended much more on the ability to finance needed imports than on the rate of domestic savings. The secular decline hypothesis, of course, implied that long-run export expansion would not necessarily break the bottleneck, nor could it be broken by short-run exchange rate policy since both exports and imports were regarded as price-inelastic. This short-run "elasticity pessimism" implied of course that the devaluations resulting from chronic balance of payments imbalances would have virtually no effect in reducing imports or in stimulating exports, so the effect would simply be to fuel domestic inflation through increases in the cost of imports. The only available option was for the country to ration its relatively inflexible foreign exchange supply for use in "essential" imports, and embark upon reducing the import content of domestic consumption through import substitution.

In addition to this, industrialization *per se*—import-substituting or otherwise—was seen as a means of absorbing the relatively abundant labor supplies of LDCs, abundant in both absolute and in relative terms, and ever more abundant as a result of the population explosion.

The actual results ran directly counter to the ostensible objectives of the policy. With regard to the import bottleneck, the central paradox of import substitution was that it resulted in an even greater dependence on imports, and greater vulnerability to adverse movements in the capacity to import. This was for two reasons. First, industrialization based on import substitution was almost by definition geared to the internal market, and hence has been foreign exchange *using* rather than foreign exchange *earning*, while the import substitution policy did nothing to stimulate exports, and in fact tended to reduce the incentive to export. Import substitution from the outset required erecting barriers to competing imports, which in practice raised the cost to users and was therefore equivalent to a subsidy to domestic import-competing producers financed by a tax on domestic consumers. The objective of trade policy was to permanently restructure internal relative prices in favor of domestic industry and against other sectors, including the agriculture and export sectors (there was, of course in many LDCs a greater or lesser degree of overlap in these sectors).

Protection, in other words, taxed agriculture and export activity as it raised the price of industrial versus agricultural and export goods in the domestic market. Thus, the profitability of exports declined with protection, and since protection raised the (domestic) price of imported goods generally, some users switched some of their domestic expenditure to the relatively cheaper exportable goods. Pressure from a lower supply and higher domestic consumption of export goods combined to reduce the overall incentive to export. It is rather ironic that this negative long-run effect of protectionism was compensated during the 1950s by unusually favorable terms of trade, and it can be argued that if the policy seemed initially successful it was largely due to this rather fortuitous circumstance.

From the import side, it became apparent that, contrary to expectations, import *substitution* did not in fact reduce the aggregate demand for imports, but only changed the *composition* of import demand. The LDCs which embarked upon import substitution reduced their demand for imported consumer goods, but increased their demand for the inputs, raw materials and capital goods with which to produce the "domestic" import-competing consumer goods. Furthermore, since these were goods which, though essential for domestic production, simply could *not* be produced within the country, the demand for them was quite insensitive to changes in price, since an interruption in their supply could bring domestic production to a standstill. The country was therefore even *more* dependent than before, and more vulnerable to adverse movements in the terms of trade, such as that which resulted from the OPEC oil price hike, probably the worst catastrophe that non-oil LDCs have had to face since the Great Depression. As Deepak Lal succinctly put it:

> The foreign-exchange shortage, which might initially have been cured by the normal means of a devaluation, was then chronic. Through the policies it engendered, the foreign-exchange gap had become a self-fulfilling prophecy by *leading* to the very retardation of export earnings and the irreducibility of minimum import requirements which were its premises.[21]

Neither did import-substituting industrialization do much toward solving the growing employment problem in the LDCs. In fact, it is well known that the industrial sector in the LDCs, while growing at a substantially faster rate than other sectors (hardly surprising in view of its favored status), has consistently failed to absorb the growing urban labor force which rapid population growth and internal migrations were making available. Growth in industrial employment in fact has lagged behind

---

[21]Deepak Lal, *The Poverty of Development Economics* (London: Institute of Economic Affairs, 1983), p. 26.

employment growth in other, less rapidly expanding sectors.[22] The reverse side of the coin to modernism and high labor productivity in industrial employment was swelling numbers of jobs in low productivity sectors, particularly in the service sector. Industry has, therefore, been capital-intensive rather than labor-using.

This has often been attributed to distortions in relative factor prices, that is, in the relative cost of capital goods as compared to labor costs. To be sure, such distortions are pervasive and widespread, and range from low and often negative real rates of interest in the credit markets to waivers of import duties and other taxes and even preferential exchange rates for imports of machinery and other capital goods. These distortions, intended to encourage investment, by lowering the cost of capital relative to that of labor have, in fact, resulted in a higher capital/labor ratio, in spite of the fact that in these countries labor is the relatively most abundant factor of production. Lewis has graphically described one of the most obvious of the resulting distortions:

> The waste [of capital] has come mainly in substituting capital for labor in moving things about; in the handling of materials inside the factory; in packaging; in mining; and in building and construction. The bulldozer, the conveyor belt, and the crane usually achieve nothing that labor could not do equally well. They spend scarce foreign exchange solely in order to produce unemployment.[23]

These distortions go a long way toward explaining the actual path of industrial development, though there is reason to believe that factor price distortions have only aggravated a problem that would have arisen even in the absence of these distortions. That is, the industrialization which took place under the aegis of the import substitution policy would have been capital-intensive anyway, and factor price distortions have only reinforced that trend.

To state a rather obvious but too often overlooked technological fact, though many products can be produced with alternative technologies that

---

[22]See W. Baer, "Import Substitution and Industrialization in Latin America: Experiences and Interpretations," *Latin American Research Review*, 7 (Spring 1972): 101-08, and D. T. Healey, "Development Policy: New Thinking About an Interpretation," *Journal of Economic Literature*, 10 (Sept 1972): 757-97. These studies are no less relevant for being somewhat dated—a decade and a half later the situation is the same, if not worse.

[23]W. A. Lewis, *Development Planning* (London: Allen & Unwin, 1966), p. 60.

differ in the relative intensity with which they employ capital and labor, some products are absolutely capital-intensive in the sense that they require a high capital/labor ratio even under the most (relatively) labor-intensive technology available, while other products are absolutely labor-intensive in the same sense. Under a regime of free trade, labor-abundant economies will tend to specialize in producing the latter type of products, and will tend to import the former.[24] Therefore, import-substituting industries in LDCs would have been obliged to adopt capital-intensive technologies even in the absence of factor price distortions, since the import-substituting products were by their nature capital-intensive. Thus, by encouraging import substitution these countries were, by their own choice, shifting their productive structure toward the production of a more capital-intensive *mix* of products.

To be sure, in the absence of distortions in factor prices even the import-substituting industries could be expected to adopt relatively labor-intensive technologies, compared to the technologies employed in developed countries, but these would still be relatively capital-intensive compared to the pre-import-substitution structure of production in the LDCs, which is the relevant comparison. Increases in output, and hence in employment, in the industrial sector were thus highly limited by the availability of capital investment, and conversely, the output and employment effects of given capital investments in industry were much less than could have been obtained by investments in more labor-intensive sectors such as agriculture or the export sector generally.

In this regard, it has become fashionable recently to lament the "inappropriate technology problem," that is, the fact that the foreign technology that LDCs must import is invariably labor-saving. Viewed in perspective, however, it should be clear that the problem is not so much one of inappropriate technologies as one of inappropriate *products*.

A Concluding Remark

Ultimately, the proponents of protectionism in LDCs have been misled by a false interpretation of a historical correlation. Historical studies of (now) developed economies show that the share of industry in total output rose during the course of their economic growth. As Meier has aptly pointed out, however, it is one thing to establish what happened during the course of development in one country, and quite another to infer from this

---

[24]In modern (ortodox?) international trade theory this proposition is known as the Heckscher-Ohlin theorem.

experience that the same result can be induced more rapidly through deliberate policy.[25] The hot-house industrialization that protection has produced at great cost in some LDCs is merely a symbol of modernity, not to be mistaken for the reality of economic development.

[25]Meier, *Leading Issues in Development Economics*, p. 298. A short but quite comprehensive survey of the evidence on the historical development of industrialization is that by J. R. T. Hughes, "Industrialization: Economic Aspects," *International Encyclopedia of the Social Sciences* (1968), vol. 7, pp. 252-63.

3

THE CONTRIBUTION OF ECONOMIC FREEDOM TO WORLD ECONOMIC GROWTH, 1980-99[1]

Since 1986, a group of researchers associated with the Fraser Institute have focused on the definition and measurement of an internationally comparable index of economic freedom (Easton and Walker, 1992; Gwartney, Block and Lawson, 1996). This work has resulted in the development of a numerical index which, in its most recent version (Gwartney *et al.*, 2002), ranks 123 countries in terms of their degree of economic freedom, as measured by a composite of 38 indicators grouped in five major categories (size of government, legal structure, monetary and banking policy, international trade, and regulation). One important finding is that the degree of economic freedom, as measured by the "Economic Freedom of the World" index (EFW), is highly correlated with both the level and the rate of growth of real per capita GDP (see Table 1).

These comparisons, though striking, nonetheless suffer from two limitations: (1) they are simple, two-variable correlations, and (2) they are average results for groupings of countries.

Analyzing the results for countries grouped in quintiles averages out much of the actual dispersion in the data, while ignoring the effect of other explanatory variables might bias the results due to an "omitted variables" effect. The purpose of this paper is to evaluate the incremental explanatory power of the EFW index in the context of more general models of economic growth. The period chosen for study was 1980-99, and the

[1]Published originally in *Cato Journal*, 23 (Fall 2003): 189-98. The author thanks Lucía Olivero, for valuable research assistance, and James Gwartney and Robert Lawson, for critical comments and help in providing some of the datasets.

Table 1. Economic Freedom, per capita Income, and Economic Growth.

Countries Ranked by EFW Index	GDP per capita 2000 PPP (us$)	Growth rate (%), per capita GDP, 1990-2000
Bottom quintile	2,556	–0.85
4th quintile	4,365	1.44
3rd quintile	6,235	1.13
2nd quintile	12,390	1.57
Top quintile	23,450	2.56

Source: Gwartney *et al.* (2002), p. 20, Exhibits 5 and 8.

growth-regressions were estimated for a sample of 106 countries. (Data sources are detailed in the Appendix.)

Convergence and Economic Freedom

At first glance, the results in Table 1 seem to contradict at least some aspects of neo-classical growth models, since the high-EFW countries are not only richer than low-EFW ones, but also grow faster, contrary to the "convergence" predictions of the standard models, which imply that high-income countries will tend to have lower rates of growth due to diminishing returns on physical capital (Solow, 1956). However, these two effects are not necessarily mutually exclusive—in principle *both* effects can hold—since, as Barro and Sala-i-Martin have pointed out, the convergence effect is actually a *ceteris paribus* prediction (Barro and Sala-i-Martin, 1992; Barro, 1994; Sala-i-Martin, 1996). What the neo-classical models predict is that, *other things equal*, countries with higher initial income will have slower growth, and vice-versa.

Therefore, a direct test of the existence of both effects would be to regress the growth rate of real per capita GDP against (1) the log of initial-year PPP-adjusted per capita GDP, (2) the EFW index, and (3) a set of additional explanatory variables, as suggested by some prior theoretical framework. The convergence effect predicts that the first variable should have a negative coefficient, and the interpretation of the regression in *ceteris paribus* terms is straightforward: other things equal, (1) if two

42

countries have the same level of economic freedom, as measured by the EFW index, the country with the higher initial income will tend to have a lower growth rate due to the convergence effect; (2) on the other hand, if two countries start out with the same income level, the country with more economic freedom will tend to grow faster.

The usefulness of the EFW index as an explanatory variable for economic growth can be evaluated by examining its performance under different model specifications. One possibility is to include EFW in a growth-regression based on the now-standard "augmented" Solow growth model (Mankiw, Romer and Weil, 1992; Knight, Loayza and Villanueva, 1993). Models following this approach usually include initial income, investment share in GDP, a measure of population growth, and some measure of human capital. Another option is to include EFW in a simplified version of a model recently proposed by Gallup, Sachs and Mellinger (1999), explaining per capita income growth in terms of the convergence effect and three "geographic" variables. Estimating the effect of EFW in the context of these two different models is a quite strong test of "robustness" for this variable, since it would be hard to imagine characterizations of the growth process that differ as much as these do. If it turns out that EFW is significant in *both* regressions, then one could conclude that economic freedom is indeed a significant factor in economic growth, regardless of one's basic theoretical framework.

Economic Freedom in a Neo-classical Growth Model

Regressions based on the neo-classical model are reported in Table 2 (Regressions 1 to 6).[2] The first regression uses only the variables in the basic model:

LOGGDP80 = log of PPP-adjusted per capita GDP in 1980,

INV = investment share in GDP, average for 1980-99,

FERTIL = total fertility rate, average for 1980-99, used as the measure of population growth,[3]

---

[2]All of the regressions in Table 2 were estimated by OLS. Numbers in brackets are t-values of the estimated coefficients. For regressions 3, 7 and 8 the t-values were estimated using the White (1980) correction.

[3]Use of the fertility rate as the measure of population growth gives a better fit in the regressions, and its coefficient is also easier to interpret. However, none of the

DSCH15 = change in "average years of schooling for the population aged 15 and over," 1980-95 (as measured by Barro and Lee, 2001), used as the human capital variable.

This model performs rather well. These four variables explain 60.6 % of the cross-country variation in economic growth over this period, and all of the variables are significant and have the expected signs.

Regression 2 adds the average EFW index for each country (measured as the average of the values for 1980, 1985, 1990, 1995). Though we lose 5 observations due to missing values, the results are still quite strong. The coefficient for EFW is positive and significant, and the explanatory power increases to 69.5 %. The coefficients for the other variables are significant and quite similar to the previous results.

Regression 3 adds DEFW, the change in the EFW index from 1980 to 1995. This too has a positive and significant coefficient, and increases the explanatory power to 74.1 %. This suggests that the growth-effect of economic freedom depends not only on the absolute *level* of the EFW index during any given period, but also on the direction (and magnitude) of the *change* in the index over that period.

Regression 4 disaggregates DSCH15 into its male and female components.[4] The results suggest that it is the male component of the schooling variable that really counts in terms of economic growth.[5] Regression 5 drops DFEMSCH15. All variables are significant (including EFW and DEFW), and the results are essentially similar to those in Regression 3.

Finally, Regression 6 replaces INV with an interaction term between INV and EFW (INV*EFW). In this regression, the effect of changes in the investment rate is conditional on the value of EFW: each one-point increase in the EFW index increases the impact of a one point increase in INV by about 0.014 percentage points. Thus, other things equal, if the investment rates in two countries differ by 10 points (say, 10 and 20 % of

---

substantive conclusions are altered by using the population growth rate instead.

[4]Figures on male schooling for 1980 and 1995 were derived from data on total and female schooling using the formula MALESCH = 2*SCH – FEMSCH.

[5]This confirms findings of other researchers in this regard (for instance, Barro, 2001), and may be due to the fact that in most countries men still account for the larger share of the labor-force. Even with current low female labor-participation rates, however, this result does not imply that female education has no effect at all on economic growth, since there is an important indirect effect due to the impact of female education on fertility levels.

GDP), on average their annual growth rates would differ by about 1.4 percentage points if EFW = 10 (very high economic freedom), but only by about 0.14 percentage points if EFW = 1 (very low economic freedom). Notice that EFW has an independent effect of its own in this regression, which implies that not all of its effect occurs through effects on investment productivity.[6] The coefficients for the other variables are quite similar to those in Regression 5, and the explanatory power is practically the same in both regressions, so there is not much reason for preferring one over the other on purely statistical grounds, though Regression 6 seems theoretically more appealing since it allows for changes in the productivity of investment as a function of the EFW index. The results imply that any given level of investment will have a higher growth impact in countries with greater degrees of economic freedom.[7]

Geography, Economic Freedom, and Growth

We can conclude, from Regressions 1 to 6, that economic freedom, as measured by the EFW index, adds significantly to the explanatory power of a neo-classical growth model.[8] To test the robustness of this finding with respect to changes in model specification, we will estimate the effect of economic freedom in the context of a growth-regression based on a totally different approach.

A series of recent studies directed by Jeffrey Sachs have focused on the relationship between geography and economic development (Gallup, Sachs and Mellinger, 1999; Sachs, 2000). The motivation for these studies

---

[6]The coefficient for EFW in Regression 6 is lower than in Regression 5, but these coefficients cannot be compared directly because in Regression 6 the effect of a unit change in EFW is conditional on INV, and now equals 0.423 + 0.0139*INV. The mean value for INV is 21.1 % of GDP for the 85 countries in the sample for Regressions 5 and 6 (for the 106 country sample it is 21.5 %). For this value of INV, the effect of a unit change in EFW would be 0.716, which is actually quite close to the estimated coefficient for EFW in Regression 5.

[7]This issue is also explored, using a slightly different methodology, in a working paper by Gwartney, Holcombe and Lawson (2003).

[8]Easton and Walker (1997), working with *levels* of income, and Dawson (1998), working with rates of growth, applied an earlier version of the EFW index to extend the results of Mankiw, Romer and Weil (1992). Both studies confirmed that addition of an economic freedom measure increases the explanatory power of the neo-classical model.

is based on two empirical observations: (1) Countries located in tropical regions of the world tend to be poor, whereas countries in temperate zones tend to be wealthier—a comparison of GDP per capita in countries grouped according to geographic latitude illustrates this tendency quite graphically (Sachs, 2000, Fig. 2), and (2) countries with easy access to maritime transportation tend to be wealthier than landlocked countries. (These two tendencies are mutually reinforcing: landlocked *and* tropical countries are in double jeopardy, and tend to be the poorest of all.)

Though these studies consider a very large number of different variables, we will concentrate here on the three main location-related variables used in Gallup, Sachs and Mellinger (1999):

TROPICAR = proportion of a country's territory located in the geographic tropics,[9]

POP100KM = proportion of the country's population living within 100 kilometers of the sea coast,

LOGDIST = log of minimum distance of the country to one of three core areas of the world economy (defined as New York, Rotterdam or Tokyo).

The Gallup, Sachs and Mellinger study found that these three variables explained a large share of the cross-country variation in real income *levels* in 1950, 1990 and 1995. In addition, it was found that the effect of these variables increased through time, implying a geographic effect on *rates of growth* as well.

To test for a geographic effect on growth in the 1980-99 sample period, we first estimate Regression 7, a growth-regression based on these three variables, plus initial income (to allow for a convergence effect). Both TROPICAR and POP100KM are significant and have the expected signs, though LOGDIST is not significant. The convergence effect, though negative, as expected, is only marginally significant. Overall explanatory power for this regression is quite low (23.9 %).

Adding EFW and DEFW to this model (Regression 8) substantially increases its explanatory power (54.3 %). All of the variables are significant (again, except for LOGDIST) with the expected signs, and it is noteworthy that in this model the estimated growth-impact of economic freedom is even stronger than in the neo-classical model.

---

[9]Tropical regions are defined as areas located between 23.5 degrees of latitude North (Tropic of Cancer) and 23.5 degrees of latitude South (Tropic of Capricorn).

Conclusions

The purpose of this paper is not to compare different theories of economic growth, but to evaluate the growth-impact of economic freedom under alternative theoretical frameworks. The particular measure of economic freedom employed—the EFW index—was found to be quite "robust" with respect to major changes in model specification. We conclude that economic freedom is a significant factor in economic growth, regardless of the basic theoretical framework.

This has important implications, since the EFW index stresses a broad set of policy-related variables that are known to directly affect economic efficiency: inflation rates, taxes, public spending, government enterprises and state-directed investment, tariff protection and non-tariff trade barriers, price controls, labor and credit market distortions, etc. The negative effects of these policy-induced distortions are almost surely mutually reinforcing and, in any case, tend to be highly correlated (countries with bad policies tend to be consistently bad along many policy dimensions), so it is hard to sort out their separate effects. It seems pretty clear, however, that consistently bad policies have a major negative impact on economic growth, while improvements in the policy mix can be significantly growth-enhancing. The EFW index provides, in effect, a report card on a country's overall economic policy (and, implicitly, suggestions on how to get a better "grade"). It is, moreover, a report card with considerable predictive power. Policy analysts would be well advised to keep an eye on this index in the future.

Appendix: Data Sources

The following data sources were used in this study:

(1) Economic and population variables: *World Development Indicators*, 2001 (CDROM version). This source reports data for 207 countries, but coverage for some of them is rather limited. For this study, the basic sample is restricted to countries for which figures are available on real GDP per capita for the years 1980 and 1999 (thus allowing calculation of a rate of growth of real per capita GDP over that sample period). This sample is reduced further to 106 countries for which full data are available on variables required for Regressions 1 and 7.

(2) Educational attainment: Barro and Lee (2001). Their dataset can be downloaded from www2.cid.Harvard.edu/ciddata/barrolee/Appendix.xls.

(3) Economic Freedom of the World Index: James Gwartney and Robert Lawson, "Chain-linked Adjusted Summary Index," Madrid Meeting of Economic Freedom Network (Oct 2002). Dataset provided by Robert Lawson.

(4) Geographic variables: Gallup, Sachs, and Mellinger (1999). Their data set can be downloaded from www2.cid.harvard.edu/ciddata/ geodata.csv.

Table 2 – Determinants of Economic Growth, 1980-99: Regression Results.

Dependent Variable: Average annual rate of growth (%), real per capita GDP, 1980-99.

Regression Number:	[1]	[2]	[3]	[4]	[5]	[6]	[7]	[8]
Constant	14.604 [5.559]	13.061 [5.189]	11.752 [3.739]	11.662 [4.953]	11.669 [4.996]	13.797 [6.506]	4.666 1.147]	1.604 [0.408]
LOGGDP80	-1.433 [-5.831]	-1.742 [-7.282]	-1.77 [-5.748]	-1.751 [-7.891]	-1.752 [-8.007]	-1.754 [-7.912]	-0.449 [-1.374]	-1.159 [-3.067]
INV	0.076 [3.035]	0.082 [2.902]	0.075 [2.613]	0.085 [3.077]	0.084 [3.288]			
INV*EFW						0.0139 [3.068]		
FERTIL	-1.203 [-7.859]	-1.091 [-7.369]	-0.999 [-5.432]	-1.002 [-7.203]	-1.002 [-7.251]	-1.037 [-7.608]		
DSCH15	0.531 [2.868]	0.568 [3.229]	0.555 [2.869]					
DMALESCH15				0.529 [2.394]	0.521 [3.649]	0.529 [3.681]		
DFEMSCH15				-0.013 [-0.050]				
EFW		0.621 [4.319]	0.789 [4.602]	0.76 [5.331]	0.761 [5.490]	0.423 [2.222]		1.245 [7.007]
DEFW			0.478 [3.378]	0.46 [3.570]	0.461 [3.616]	0.458 [3.566]		0.715 [3.955]
TROPICAR							-2.148 [-3.767]	-2.333 [-4.132]
POP100KM							2.095 [3.768]	1.293 [2.462]
LOGDIST							-0.007 [-0.033]	0.217 [1.047]
R-squared	0.606	0.695	0.741	0.746	0.746	0.742	0.239	0.543
N	90	85	85	85	85	85	96	87
White test (chi-square)	5.03	24.928	40.653	43.281	38.83	38.265	27.753	48.996
d.f. for White test	14	20	27	35	27	27	14	27
prob-value	0.985	0.204	0.044	0.159	0.066	0.074	0.015	0.006

REFERENCES

Barro, R. J. (1994) *Economic Growth and Convergence*. Occasional Papers No. 46. San Francisco: International Center for Economic Growth.

————. (2001) "Human Capital and Growth." *American Economic Review*, 91 (May): 12-17.

Barro, R. J. and J.-W. Lee. (2001) "International Data on Educational Attainment: Updates and Implications." *Oxford Economic Papers*, 53 (July): 541-63.

Barro, R. J. and X. Sala-i-Martin. (1992) "Convergence." *Journal of Political Economy*, 100 (April): 223-51.

Dawson, J. W. (1998) "Institutions, Investment and Growth: New Cross-Country and Panel Data Evidence." *Economic Inquiry*, 36 (Oct): 603-19.

Easton, S. T. and M. A. Walker, eds. (1992) *Rating Global Economic Freedom*. Vancouver: Fraser Institute.

————. (1997) "Income, Growth, and Economic Freedom." *American Economic Review*, 87 (May): 328-32.

Gallup, J. L., J. D. Sachs and A. D. Mellinger. (1999) "Geography and Economic Development." *Annual World Bank Conference on Development Economics 1998*, pp. 127-70. Washington: World Bank.

Gwartney, J. D., W. E. Block and R. A. Lawson. (1996) *Economic Freedom of the World: 1975-1995*. Vancouver: Fraser Institute.

Gwartney, J. D., *et al.* (2002) *Economic Freedom of the World—2002 Annual Report*. Vancouver: Fraser Institute.

Gwartney, J. D., R. G. Holcombe and R. A. Lawson. (2003) "Economic Freedom, Institutional Quality, and Cross-Country Differences in Income and Growth." Unpublished manuscript.

Knight, M., N. Loayza and D. Villanueva. (1993) "Testing the Neoclassical Theory of Economic Growth." *IMF Staff Papers*, 40 (Sept): 512-41.

Mankiw, N. G., D. Romer and D. N. Weil. (1992) "A Contribution to the Empirics of Economic Growth." *Quarterly Journal of Economics*, 107 (May): 407-37.

Sachs, J. D. (2000) "Tropical Underdevelopment." CID Working Paper No. 57. Center for International Development, Harvard University (Dec).

Sala-i-Martin, X. (1996) "The Classical Approach to Convergence Analysis." *Economic Journal*, 106 (July): 1019-36.

Solow, R. M. (1956) "A Contribution to the Theory of Economic Growth." *Quarterly Journal of Economics*, 70 (Feb): 65-94.

White, H. (1980) "A Heteroskedasticity-Consistent Covariance Matrix Estimator and a Direct Test for Heteroskedasticity." *Econometrica*, 48 (May): 817–38.

4

HANDLING ECONOMIC FREEDOM IN GROWTH REGRESSIONS: SUGGESTIONS FOR CLARIFICATION

Introduction

A recent exchange between Lawson (2006) and de Haan and Sturm (2006) highlights an important methodological issue in empirical studies of the connection between economic freedom (*EF*) and economic growth.

In a major survey article on the measurement and applications of economic freedom indicators (de Haan, Lundström and Sturm, 2006), the authors criticized, among other things, the tendency in many applied studies to use both the level *and* the change in the *EF* index as regressors in cross-country growth-regressions, advocating instead a specification in which only the *change* in the *EF* index is included. In their view, "studies that jointly employ the level and the change of EF as regressors are suspect" (p. 177).[1]

In his comment, Lawson argues that using the level of the *EF* index (in addition to the change over time) should not be ruled out *a priori*, but should be decided empirically. He also makes a strong theoretical case for including both the level *and* the change in *EF* in an initial equation specification. The purpose of this note is to help clarify some of the issues involved in this discussion.

Co-authored with Robert A. Lawson. Published originally in *Econ Journal Watch*, 4 (1) (2007): 71-78.

[1] Full disclosure: Both authors have published papers that de Haan *et al.* criticize in this regard.

The Specification Issue

Consider the following specifications:

(1) $$GROWTH = a_0 + a_1 EF_0 + a_2 \Delta EF + a_3 Z$$

(2) $$GROWTH = b_0 + b_1 EF_0 + b_2 EF_1 + b_3 Z$$

(3) $$GROWTH = c_0 + c_1 EF_1 + c_2 Z$$

(4) $$GROWTH = d_0 + d_1 \Delta EF + d_2 Z$$

where $GROWTH$ is the rate of economic growth over some period, EF_0 is the economic freedom index at the beginning of the period, EF_1 is the economic freedom index at the end of the period, Z is a matrix of control variables (i.e., other variables affecting $GROWTH$ over the period), and $\Delta EF = EF_1 - EF_0$ by definition. Equation (1) is Lawson's preferred specification, while de Haan et al. favor Equation (4).

The theoretical case for Equation (1) is straightforward: (a) If EF matters at all for economic growth, then we would expect that, other things equal (i.e., holding ΔEF and the Z variables constant), countries with higher initial levels of EF should grow faster than countries with lower initial levels. This would show up as a positive and significant estimate for a_1 in Equation (1). (b) On the other hand, two countries might have the same initial values for EF (and similar values for the Z variables), except that in one country EF is increasing over the sample period ($\Delta EF > 0$) while in the other it is decreasing ($\Delta EF < 0$). In that case, and if EF indeed matters for growth, then we would expect the former country to have better economic performance than the latter. This would show up as a positive and significant estimate for a_2 in Equation (1).

Both Lawson and de Haan et al. agree that $a_2 > 0$. The difference is in the treatment of a_1. Lawson favors including EF_0 in the regression (and predicts that $a_1 > 0$), while de Haan et al. insist on excluding EF_0 (thereby implicitly assuming that $a_1 = 0$).[2]

---

[2] It is not entirely clear that de Haan et al. actually believe that initial EF has no impact on growth whatsoever, or whether their favored approached is premised exclusively on grounds of econometric methodology.

Given that $\Delta EF = EF_1 - EF_0$, Equation (2) is formally identical to Equation (1), with $b_1 = a_1 - a_2$ and $b_2 = a_2$. There is no difference between estimating (1) or (2). Estimated coefficients for the two regressions will satisfy these relationships, while the constant and the coefficients for the other regressors will be identical in both regressions, as well as the R^2 and other regression statistics. The only difference is in the standard error for b_1, the coefficient for EF_0 in Equation (2), which is of course related to the results for Equation (1) by

$$Var(b_1) = Var(a_1 - a_2) = Var(a_1) + Var(a_2) - 2Cov(a_1, a_2)$$

where $Var(b_1)$ is the sample variance for b_1, $Var(a_1)$ and $Var(a_2)$ are the sample variances for a_1 and a_2 from Equation (1), and $Cov(a_1, a_2)$ is the covariance between a_1 and a_2. From a strictly econometric point of view there is nothing to choose between these two regressions, because *they are the same regression.*

There seems to be some confusion about this point when Lawson writes:

> I agree that Equation (2) is still a problematic specification because the level of *EF* at the beginning of the period is likely to be highly collinear with the level of *EF* at the end of the period. This high degree of collinearity between EF_0 and EF_1 will make the coefficient estimates in Equation (2) difficult to interpret and will bias the standard errors (p. 403).

Equation (2) might indeed be more difficult to interpret, but only because it is a somewhat unorthodox way to express Equation (1), and not because of collinearity or any other statistical problems present in (2) but not in (1).[3] If classical OLS assumptions are satisfied in one equation, they will also be satisfied in the other, and both equations will yield unbiased estimates of their respective coefficients.[4]

---

[3]Lawson agrees entirely with this. The primary point was that Equation (2) is simply difficult to interpret economically relative to Equation (1).

[4]If a_1 and a_2 are about the same order of magnitude, then b_1 in Equation (2) might be small (or even negative). At first glance, one might think that this is due to the fact that $EF_1 = EF_0 + \Delta EF$, and therefore EF_0 does not add any additional information to the regression. This is not, however, a matter of statistics, but of simple numerics. The results for EF_0 in Equation (2) depend upon the sign of the coefficient for ΔEF in Equation (1). If, in some other context, ΔEF happened to

The fact that (1) and (2) are formally identical seems to be the essence of the de Haan-Sturm case against including the level of EF in a growth-regression. Their argument is, in effect, a two-step one: First discredit (2), and then discredit (1) by implication.

The problem, in their view, is that (2) includes EF_1, the value of EF at the end of the sample period. To understand why they think this is a problem, first consider Equation (3), in which $GROWTH$ depends upon end-period EF but not upon initial EF. For some reason, there seems to be unanimous agreement that (3) is an inadmissible specification. Lawson states:

> Clearly, [Equation (3)] is inappropriate as it is logically impossible for the level of economic freedom at the end of the period to affect economic growth in the previous period. Something occurring today cannot determine what happened yesterday (p. 402).

And de Haan-Sturm concur:

> We all agree that [Equation (3)] does not make theoretical sense: the level of economic freedom at the end of the sample period cannot explain economic growth experienced over the sample (p. 409).

But is it really true that (3) is "logically impossible" and "does not make theoretical sense"? After all, EF_1 is simply EF_0 plus ΔEF, so (3) equals

$$GROWTH = c_0 + c_1 EF_0 + c_1 \Delta EF + c_2 Z$$

and is therefore simply a restricted version of Equation (1) with $a_1 = a_2$. Thus, (3) simply states that a one-unit cross-country difference in initial EF and a one-unit cross-country difference in ΔEF have the same effect on $GROWTH$. Now, this restriction seems arbitrary, and might well be an invalid assumption, but that does not make it somehow "nonsensical," and in any case it is something that should be decided empirically, not on theoretical grounds.[5]

---

have a negative coefficient in a regression similar in form to Equation (1), then EF_0 would have a "large" coefficient in the equivalent Equation (2) form. In any case, the fact that EF_0 has a small (or negative) coefficient in Equation (2) does not imply that this variable has a small (or negative) effect on $GROWTH$, since the full effect of cross-country differences in EF_0 equals $b_1 + b_2$ ($= a_1$ in Equation (1)).

[5]Lawson now concedes that the problem isn't the logical invalidity of (3) but rather its statistical invalidity in that the implied restriction cannot be supported

Nor is the de Haan-Sturm "solution" any better, since Equation (4) can be expressed as:

$$GROWTH = d_0 - d_1 EF_0 + d_1 EF_1 + d_2 Z$$

which, as Lawson rightly notes (p. 404), is simply a restricted version of Equation (2) with $b_1 = -b_2$. Thus, if de Haan-Sturm reject Equation (2)—and by implication, Equation (1)—because it includes EF_1 as a regressor, then they should reject their own preferred equation as well, since it includes EF_1 too.

The point is that the proper specification for a growth regression that includes economic freedom should be driven first by theory, and any restrictions placed on the regression should be subject to empirical testing. We still maintain that the de Haan-Sturm specification implies a restriction that cannot be justified statistically and that the omission of the level of EF represents a potentially serious omitted variable problem.

The Endogeneity Issue

To be fair, we are perhaps talking at cross-purposes here. Lawson's primary issue in his comment was about the proper *specification* of the growth regression. De Haan-Sturm in contrast make much of *reverse-causation* and *endogeneity*—issues that affect all cross-country growth regressions of the sort de Haan, Lundström and Sturm (2006) originally surveyed. The problem is that a strong empirical correlation between, say, *GROWTH* and ΔEF, does not necessarily imply that the direction of causality is $\Delta EF \rightarrow GROWTH$, since it could be the other way around (reverse-causality), or both ΔEF and *GROWTH* could be responding to some other factor (endogeneity).

What we fail to see is why this should be less of a problem in Equation (4) than in the other three specifications since ΔEF (and implicitly EF_0 and EF_1) is in Equation (4) as well. If there is a reverse-causality problem in Equation (1) or (2), then it is likely still to be present in Equation (4). Dropping a single variable, EF_0, is not likely to eliminate magically any reverse-causality or endogeneity problems associated with ΔEF and *GROWTH*.

If reverse-causality and/or endogeneity are the real bone of contention,

---

with standard statistical testing.

then we see three solutions, each with problems of their own. (1) We could discard ΔEF altogether and estimate a model containing only the initial-period EF; after all nobody is suggesting that economic growth over the sample period somehow "determines" initial EF. The problem here, however, is that if Equation (1) is really the true model, as Lawson suggests, then discarding ΔEF will create an omitted variable problem, biasing the estimated coefficient for EF_0. (2) We could use the level of EF and the ΔEF from a period *before* the growth period under investigation to test for reverse causality (see for example, Gwartney *et al.*, 2006). This approach faces data limitations and still fails to account for possible endogeneity. (3) We could dispense with single-equation estimation altogether and move to an instrumental variables (IV) approach. While this method may deal with the problem, IV models themselves invite a whole host of criticisms in terms of what the proper instruments should be, and the results themselves are especially fragile to the choice of instruments.

Endogeneity and reverse-causation are, to be sure, important and thorny issues, but they are present in practically any kind of econometric analysis, especially in these reduced-form cross-country growth regressions. Indeed, that "correlation does not imply causation" is something that statisticians and econometricians have known for ages and not something that we all suddenly realized after we learned how to say "endogeneity." This just means that regression models only provide measures of the degree of statistical association between variables, and that inferences regarding causality require an *interpretation* of the results in terms of prior theory. Econometric technique *per se* will often provide little guidance in this respect, especially in the kind of cross-section studies we are concerned with here.

REFERENCES

De Haan, Jakob, Susanna Lundström and Jan-Egbert Sturm. 2006. "Market-Oriented Institutions and Policies and Economic Growth: A Critical Survey." *Journal of Economic Surveys*, 20 (2): 157-181.

De Haan, Jakob and Jan-Egbert Sturm. 2006. "How to Handle Economic Freedom: Reply to Lawson." *Econ Journal Watch*, 3 (3): 407-410.

Gwartney, James, Randall Holcombe, and Robert Lawson. 2006. "Institutions and the Impact of Investment on Growth." *Kyklos,* 59 (2): 255-76.

Lawson, Robert A. 2006. "On Testing the Connection between Economic Freedom and Growth." *Econ Journal Watch*, 3 (3): 398-406.

III. THE UNEASY CASE FOR PATENTS AND COPYRIGHTS

5

Patents and Copyrights:
Do the Benefits Exceed the Costs?

> *... it seems to me highly desirable that liberals shall strongly disagree on these topics, the more the better. What is needed more than anything else is that these questions of a policy for a competitive order should once again become live issues which are being discussed publicly; and we shall have made an important contribution if we succeed in directing interest to them.*[1]

> *The greatest constraint on your future liberties may come not from government but from corporate legal departments laboring to protect by force what can no longer be protected by practical efficiency or general social consent.*[2]

1. Introduction.

Patents and copyrights are special forms of immaterial "property" that grant to their owners the exclusive right to control the production and sale of a specified product—a literary or artistic work in the case of copyrights, an invention or productive process in the case of patents. Often these

Published originally in *Journal of Libertarian Studies*, 15 (4) (2001): 79-105. An earlier version of this paper was presented at the General Meeting of the Mont Pèlerin Society (Santiago, Chile, November 16, 2000).

[1]F. A. Hayek, "'Free' Enterprise and Competitive Order," in *Individualism and Economic Order* (Chicago: University of Chicago Press, 1948), p. 112.

[2]John Perry Barlow, "Selling Wine without Bottles: The Economy of Mind on the Global Net", in Peter Ludlow (ed.), *High Noon on the Electronic Frontier: Conceptual Issues in Cyberspace* (Cambridge, MA: MIT Press, 1996), p. 13.

concepts are subsumed under a broader concept of "intellectual property," but they are not completely analogous and cannot always be justified with the same arguments. The term "intellectual property" also covers some other very different concepts, such as trademarks. Unfortunately, in recent discussions of these topics the concept of "intellectual property" is often used generically, blurring some very important practical distinctions.[3] The purpose of this paper is to examine patents and copyrights in some detail, in order to investigate their economic effects and determine to what extent they are compatible with the principles of a free society.[4]

2. Patents as Property.

Although the term "intellectual property" is commonly used in the legal field, in economics it is rather problematic, since it is difficult to

---

[3]A trademark is a sign or label that distinguishes a given manufacturer's products from those of others. The trademark, once registered in a public registry, grants to its owner exclusive rights over its use. This guarantees the source of the product endorsed by the trademark, allowing consumers to buy with greater certainty (since the owners of well-known trademarks will have incentives to protect their value by maintaining quality standards for their products), and protecting manufacturers against forgeries (i.e., competitors trying to sell their own products by taking advantage of the good reputation of well-known trademarks). A trademark identifies the source of a product, but does not prohibit the manufacture of similar (or even identical) products, and therefore does not have the monopolistic character of the patent: If I decide to manufacture and sell "Chivas Regal" whisky I would be breaking the law, but that does not mean I cannot manufacture and sell whisky, as long as I do not use someone else's trademark. The existence of a patent, on the other hand, prevents me from producing and selling the patented product. For this reason, many people who accept the protection of trademarks as perfectly legitimate and of vital importance in a modern capitalist economy, nonetheless oppose patents on the grounds that they constitute monopoly privileges.

[4]This paper approaches the problem from an essentially utilitarian, cost-benefit perspective, and will therefore deal only indirectly with arguments premised on rights-based considerations. An excellent discussion of intellectual property issues from a non-utilitarian, rights-based perspective is that by N. Stephan Kinsella, "Against Intellectual Property," *Journal of Libertarian Studies*, 15 (Spring 2001): 1-54. See also Tom G. Palmer, "Are Patents and Copyrights Morally Justified?," *Harvard Journal of Law and Public Policy*, 13 (Summer 1990): 817–65, and "Intellectual Property: A Non-Posnerian Law and Economics Approach," *Hamline Law Review*, 12 (Spring 1989): 261–304.

justify this type of property right with the same arguments that are used to justify private property in tangible goods.

According to the economic theory of property (following David Hume), society benefits from the delimitation and protection of private property rights because goods are scarce. There is no point in defining property rights over goods when these exist in abundance. On the other hand, when goods are scarce and property is communal, they are not used efficiently. Private property guarantees that scarce goods will be put to their most efficient and productive uses.

It is difficult to justify intellectual property rights under this concept of property, since these rights do not arise from the scarcity of the appropriated objects—rather, their purpose is to *create* a scarcity, thereby generating a monopoly rent for the holders of these rights: here the law does not protect property over a scarce good, since the "scarcity" is created by the law itself, and this "artificial" scarcity is the source of the monopoly rents that confer value upon those rights. The big difference between patents and copyrights, and titles of property over tangible goods, is that the latter will be scarce even if there are no well-defined property rights, whereas in the case of patents and copyrights the scarcity only arises after the property right is defined.[5]

Defenders of patents often try to deny that they constitute monopoly privileges, arguing that the term "monopoly" is inapplicable in this case.[6] This is partly a semantic issue, although in any event there is no contradiction or incompatibility between the notions of "patent as property" and "patent as monopoly," and in practice they are closely related since the monopolistic nature of patents is precisely what confers economic value upon them.[7] Obviously, like any other monopoly

---

[5]In this century, perhaps the clearest statement of this argument is due to the English economist Arnold Plant, in a 1934 paper entitled "The Economic Theory Concerning Patents for Inventions" (reprinted in *Selected Economic Essays and Addresses* [London: Routledge & Kegan Paul, 1974], pp. 35-56). On Plant's economic thought see R. H. Coase, "Professor Sir Arnold Plant: His Ideas and Influence," in M. J. Anderson (ed.), *The Unfinished Agenda: Essays on the Political Economy of Government Policy in Honour of Arthur Seldon* (London: Institute of Economic Affairs, 1986), pp. 81-90.

[6]For instance, Michael Novak, *The Fire of Invention* (Lanham, MD: Rowman & Littlefield, 1997), pp. 69, 144.

[7]"A patent serves a fourfold purpose. Viewed morally and socially, and perhaps psychologically, it is a reward for unusual inventive ability. From the standpoint of economics and commercial law, it is a property right. Neither of these

privilege, patents can be very valuable for their owners, though that is not in itself a good reason to justify concessions of that sort. Here the relevant questions are: What implications do patents have for efficiency in the allocation of resources, and why would society want to award privileges

---

purposes—the reward to the inventor or the creation of a property right—have any restrictive economic effect in and of themselves. But then we come to the patent's third phase—from the vantage point of the state, a patent is a grant of a monopoly to the inventor based on the public interest in promoting the growth and diffusion of technology. *It is the monopoly grant that makes tangible the inventor's reward and converts a formal into a realistic property right.* Moreover, the monopoly grant has a *prima facie* impact on trade, because the monopoly conferred by the patent is the right to exclude others from manufacturing or selling the patented product, or from practicing the patented process" (Sigmund Timberg, "The Effect of the European Common Market on Anti-Trust and Patent Policy," in Crawford Shaw, ed., *Legal Problems in International Trade and Investment* [Yale Law School, 1962], p. 72, italics added)—cf., the following comments by F. A. Hayek: "The problem of the prevention of monopoly and the preservation of competition is raised much more acutely in certain other fields to which the concept of property has been extended only in recent times. I am thinking here of the extension of the concept of property to such rights and privileges as patents for inventions, copyright, trade-marks, and the like. It seems to me beyond doubt that in these fields a slavish application of the concept of property as it has been developed for material things has done a great deal to foster the growth of monopoly and that here drastic reforms may be required if competition is to be made to work. In the field of industrial patents in particular we shall have to seriously examine whether the award of a monopoly privilege is really the most appropriate and effective form of reward for the kind of risk-bearing which investment in scientific research involves. Patents, in particular, are specially interesting from our point of view because they provide so clear an illustration of how it is necessary in all instances not to apply a ready-made formula but to go back to the rationale of the market system and to decide for each class what the precise rights are to be which the government ought to protect. This is a task at least as much for economists as for lawyers. Perhaps it is not a waste of your time if I illustrate what I have in mind by quoting a rather well-known decision in which an American judge argued that 'as to the suggestion that competitors were excluded from the use of the patent we answer that such exclusion may be said to have been the very essence of the right conferred by the patent' and adds 'as it is the privilege of any owner of property to use it or not to use it without any question of motive' [*Continental Bag Co. v. Eastern Bag Co.*, 210 U.S. 405 (1909)]. It is this last statement which seems to me significant for the way in which a mechanical extension of the property concept by lawyers has done so much to create undesirable and harmful privilege"—*op. cit.*, pp. 113-14 (see also F. A. Hayek, *The Fatal Conceit* [Chicago: University of Chicago Press, 1988], pp. 36-37).

of this sort to some of its members? How does society benefit from the existence of patents? Why should society grant any special protection over the production and sale of certain products beyond that which is implied in the protection of trademarks?

Though the literature on patents often stresses inventors' rights, a perusal of the relevant legislation clearly shows that it also embodies a strong presumption that awarding patents for invention favors the public interest as well. The first formal patent law was that of the United States, passed in 1790 and based on a provision of the new Constitution of 1787, which in its enumeration of the powers vested in Congress, included the power "to promote the Progress of Science and useful Arts, by securing for limited Times to Authors and Inventors the exclusive Right to their respective Writings and Discoveries" (Art. I, Sec. 8, paragraph 8). In view of this, it is certainly interesting that from the very beginning there was never any real consensus over the benefits of adopting a patent system. Some of the most prominent drafters of the U. S. Constitution (among them several outstanding inventors) were opposed to the idea, sometimes vehemently. Among them, we can mention Benjamin Franklin, who refused the offer of a patent in his favor for the invention of his famous stove: " ... as we enjoy great advantages from the inventions of others, we should be glad of an opportunity to serve others by any invention of ours; and this we should do freely and generously."[8]

Although patents of invention originated in Europe, there was no consensus there in the recent past either. In fact, during the 19th century there was a very intense debate on the subject, especially in the quarter century between 1850 and 1875, and at one point the victory of the anti-patent movement seemed quite likely. The eventual triumph of the pro-patent position in the legislative arena reflects a political victory, but not necessarily an intellectual victory.[9]

---

[8]*The Autobiography of Benjamin Franklin*, Harvard Classics, vol. 1 (New York: P. F. Collier & Son, 1909), p. 112. Thomas Jefferson was also opposed to patents—see, for instance, his "Letter to Isaac McPherson (August 13, 1813)," in Merrill D. Peterson (ed.), *The Portable Thomas Jefferson* (New York: Viking Press, 1975). For a detailed discussion of Jefferson's views see Hugo A. Meier, "Thomas Jefferson and a Democratic Technology," in C. W. Pursell (ed.), *Technology in America* (Cambridge: MIT Press, 1990), pp. 17-33.

[9]For a history of this now-forgotten debate and a very detailed survey of the voluminous English, German and French literature that it generated, see Fritz Machlup and Edith T. Penrose, "The Patent Controversy in the Nineteenth Century," *Journal of Economic History*, 10 (May 1950): 1-29.

3. Patents and Technical Progress.

Modern defenders of the patent system, dazzled by the wonders of modern technology, never cease to stress the need to stimulate further technological development. Often cited in this context are the famous pioneer studies by Robert Solow and Edward Denison on the importance of technical progress for the explanation of economic growth.[10] The manner in which these studies are cited, however, is intriguing. These citations are made in a very general manner, and one gets the impression that authors that resort to this tactic want to attribute the *entirety* of said technical progress to patented inventions. The fact, however, is that the notion of "technical progress" in Solow-Denison type studies is a very broad category that covers, in principle, any increase in production that cannot be attributed directly to increases in the use of inputs or basic factors of production—i.e., it is equivalent to what we describe nowadays as "total factor productivity." This includes not only the effect of new technologies (not all of which represents patented inventions), but also the effects of economies of scale, and of improvements in the quality of the labor force, including better education (Denison tries to isolate the effect of education), health and nutritional levels of the labor force, and even changes in its demographic make-up. Thus, it would be short-sighted to attribute "technical progress" entirely to technological innovation *per se*. But even discounting the very important role of education and other improvements in the quality of the labor force, to attribute the residual effect entirely to a *certain type* of technological innovation (patented inventions) would be like attributing the effect of "education" entirely to formal instruction as imparted in schools (an error that is also quite common). The fact of the matter, however—and contrary to what is assumed in the pro-patents literature—is that patented inventions account for only a fraction of relevant productivity growth. Zvi Griliches, a leading expert on the study of productivity, is quite explicit on this point:

> ... not all of productivity growth is due to invention and only some fraction of the latter arises from patented inventions. If one takes 1.5 to 2.0 percent as the approximate growth rate per year in total factor

---

[10]For instance, Robert M. Sherwood, *Intellectual Property and Economic Development* (Boulder: Westview Press, 1990), pp. 82-83. The studies cited are Robert M. Solow, "Technical Change and the Aggregate Production Function," *Review of Economics and Statistics*, 39 (1957): 312-20, and Edward F. Denison, *Accounting for Slower Economic Growth* (Washington: Brookings Institution, 1979).

productivity, at least half of it is likely to be due to the growth in the quality of the labor force, economies of scale, and various allocations of capital between assets and industries. Moreover, it is unlikely that patented inventions could account for more than half of the relevant advances in knowledge. This leaves us with at most a quarter of total productivity growth, and an unknown fraction of its fluctuations, to be attributed to patented invention.[11]

Even this probably overstates the net effect of patents, since in principle we would like to estimate the *marginal* benefits derived from the existence of patents, i.e., the inventions that would not have been produced without them. Since patent protection increases the average return on inventive activity devoted to patentable inventions, thereby inducing more activity of this kind, it seems safe to conclude that the elimination of patent protection would probably adversely affect production of this type of inventions. But what would be the magnitude of that loss? We cannot just assume that *all* patented inventions are due to the existence of patents, since many of them would have been developed even without that incentive.[12] On the other hand, it certainly seems reasonable to assume that

---

[11]Zvi Griliches, "Patent Statistics as Economic Indicators: A Survey," *Journal of Economic Literature*, 28 (1990): 1699.

[12]There is not much agreement among economic historians regarding the importance of patents as a factor in the Industrial Revolution. T. S. Ashton thought that patents were unimportant ("It is at least possible that without the apparatus of the patent system discovery might have developed quite as rapidly as it did," *The Industrial Revolution, 1760-1830* [Oxford University Press, 1948], p. 11), and Joel Mokyr expresses a similar view ("A patent system may have been a stimulus to invention, but it was clearly not a necessary factor," *The Lever of Riches: Technological Creativity and Economic Progress* [Oxford University Press, 1990], p. 177). On the other hand, Douglass North argues that patents had a significant impact: "The failure to develop systematic property rights in innovation up until fairly modern times was a major source of the slow pace of technological change .... a systematic set of incentives to encourage technological change and raise the private rate of return on innovation ... was established only with the patent system .... In the absence of property rights over innovation, the pace of technological change was most fundamentally influenced by the size of markets. Other things equal, the private return upon innovation rose with larger markets. An increase in the rate of technological change in the past was associated with eras of economic expansion. In summary, economic historians of the Industrial Revolution have concentrated upon technological change as the main dynamic factor of the period. Generally, however, they have failed to ask what caused the rate of technological change to increase during this period: often, it

patents must have *some* effect on technological innovation, which is confirmed by the theoretical models, but again the interesting question is the practical magnitude of this effect.[13] In this regard, the predictions of the formal models stand in striking contrast to the available empirical evidence: although the effect is theoretically important, the results of the few studies that have tried to detect it empirically do not favor the pro-patents position. Edwin Mansfield directed two important studies on this topic in the 1980s. The first one studied 31 patented innovations in four industries (chemicals, pharmaceuticals, electronics, and machinery). One of the purposes of the study was to answer a very simple question: What proportion of innovations would be delayed or not introduced at all if they could not be patented?

---

would appear that in arguing the causes of technological progress they assume that technological progress was costless or was spontaneously generated. But in sum, an increase in the rate of technological progress will result from either an increase in the size of the market or an increase in the inventor's ability to capture a larger share of the benefits created by his invention" (*Structure and Change in Economic History* [New York: Norton, 1981], pp. 164-66). North is quick to point out, however, that "It would of course be misleading to put too much stress on a single law .... More important than patent law per se is the development and enforcement of a body of impersonal law protecting and enforcing contracts in which property rights are specified" (p. 165). Again, it is important to stress that technological change is not the only source of productivity growth (and sometimes not even the major source). Interestingly enough, North goes on to cite his own study of productivity change in ocean shipping ("Sources of Productivity Change in Ocean Shipping, 1600-1850," *Journal of Political Economy*, 76 [Sept/Oct 1968]: 953-70), which found that the major sources of the rise in total factor productivity over the 2½ centuries from 1600 to 1850 were not primarily technological developments, but rather the decline of piracy (allowing ships to reduce manpower and armament, and also lowering insurance costs), more voyages per ship per year (due, not so much to increased speed, but to less average port time per ship), and an increased load factor on return trips. The interesting thing to note in this context is that none of these important sources of productivity change were primarily technological in nature. In North's own words: " ... declining transaction costs—a result of reduced piracy, increases in size of ships, growing trade, and reduced turnaround time—led to substantial productivity growth beginning (at least) 150 years before the Industrial Revolution; and they, *more than technological change*, were responsible for productivity increases" (*Structure and Change*, p. 166, italics added).

[13]Most modern formal models follow the "Nordhaus-Scherer model"—see F. M. Scherer, "Nordhaus' Theory of Optimal Patent Life: A Geometric Interpretation," *American Economic Review*, 62 (June 1972): 422-27.

To shed light on this question, we asked each innovating firm whether it would have introduced each of its patented innovations in our sample if patent protection had not been available .... According to the firms, about one-half of the patented innovations in our sample would not have been introduced without patent protection. The bulk of these innovations occurred in the drug industry. *Excluding drug innovations, the lack of patent protection would have affected less than one-fourth of the patented innovations in our sample.*[14]

The results of the second study were even more negative:

According to detailed data obtained from a random sample of 100 firms from 12 manufacturing industries, patent protection was judged to be essential for the development or introduction of one-third or more of the inventions during 1981-83 in only 2 industries—pharmaceuticals and chemicals. On the other hand, in 7 industries (electrical equipment, office equipment, motor vehicles, instruments, primary metals, rubber, and textiles), patent protection was estimated to be essential for the development and introduction of less than 10 percent of their inventions. Indeed, in office equipment, motor vehicles, rubber, and textiles, the firms were unanimous in reporting that patent protection was not essential for the development or introduction of *any* of their inventions during this period.[15]

A more recent paper by Sakakibara and Branstetter,[16] which approaches the problem from a slightly different angle, also fails to support the pro-patents position. If patents do indeed stimulate innovation, then presumably stronger patent protection should induce a higher rate of innovation. The authors addressed the question "Do Stronger Patents Induce More Innovation?" by studying the impact of a significant Japanese

---

[14]Edwin Mansfield, Mark Schwartz and Samuel Wagner, "Imitation Costs and Patents: An Empirical Study," *Economic Journal*, 91 (Dec 1981): 915, italics added.

[15]Edwin Mansfield, "The R&D Tax Credit and Other Technology Policy Issues," *American Economic Review*, 76 (May 1986): 193. On the other hand, as Mansfield points out, "this does not mean that firms patent only a small percentage of their patentable inventions. On the contrary, they seem to patent about 50 to 80 percent of them, which is testimony to their belief that the prospective benefits from patent protection ... frequently exceed its costs."

[16]Mariko Sakakibara and Lee Branstetter, "Do Stronger Patents Induce More Innovation? Evidence from the 1988 Japanese Patent Law Reforms" (Working Paper 7066, National Bureau of Economic Research, April 1999).

patent law reform implemented in 1988. The main finding was that "the average response in terms of additional R&D effort and innovative output was quite modest." An econometric analysis using Japanese and U. S. patent data on 307 Japanese firms confirmed that the magnitude of the response was quite small.

4. Costs of the Patent System.[17]

The benefits of patents, therefore, are not as large as one might assume at first glance. On the other hand, if these benefits were costless—if patents involved a sort of "free lunch"—then there would be no reason for complaint. The fact, however, is that there are several important costs that tend to be overlooked. Apart from the considerable administrative cost and the legal expenses associated with patent litigation,[18] perhaps the most obvious economic cost of a patent system is that, in order to create incentives for the production of inventions that otherwise would not have been developed, patents create monopoly privileges over inventions that would have been developed even without the incentive. However, there are also other important costs to consider:

(1) In practice, the patent system often hinders technical progress. In the automobile industry, for instance, Henry Ford did not own the patent over the automobile, and had to fight against the owners of the patent, who constituted a closed cartel and were not interested in mass production of inexpensive models.[19] Another interesting case is the

---

[17]A recent paper by Pierre Desrochers, "On the Abuse of Patents as Economic Indicators," *Quarterly Journal of Austrian Economics*, 1 (Winter 1998): 51-74, provides a somewhat more extended discussion of the subject covered by this section, and arrives at conclusions substantially similar to those reported here.

[18]"Legal fees during the 14-year long [Kodak-Polaroid] court battle cost Kodak ... $100 million" (Kevin G. Rivette and David Kline, "Discovering New Value in Intellectual Property," *Harvard Business Review*, 78 [Jan-Feb 2000]: 65).

[19]"At the time the Ford Motor Company was organized, the automobile industry was dominated by the Association of Licensed Automobile Manufacturers (ALAM), a select group of makers of gasoline automobiles who were attempting to monopolize automobile manufacturing in the United States through control of a patent on the gasoline automobile that had been awarded in 1895 to George B. Selden, a New York patent attorney. The ALAM companies ... were in the main committed to high unit profits through producing high-priced cars for a limited

early history of aviation.[20] Inordinately broad patents are especially problematic.[21] A recent example has occurred in the field of "bio-

---

market. The ALAM tried to set production quotas and to freeze new entrances into automobile manufacturing. Henry Ford was denied a license ... under the Selden patent on the ground that he had not demonstrated his competence, and when Ford persisted in producing cars, the ALAM immediately brought a lawsuit against him for infringement of the Selden patent. The suit was ultimately decided in Ford's favor in 1911 and the ALAM disintegrated" (James J. Flink, "Henry Ford and the Triumph of the Automobile," in C. W. Pursell, ed., *Technology in America* [Cambridge: MIT Press, 1990], pp. 181-82).

[20]"Orville and Wilbur Wright ... mimicked the wing twisting of gliding birds by constructing a mechanism that warped the horizontal plane of an airplane's wings at either side in opposite directions. They patented this mechanism and claimed in their patent that their rights extended to any system that varied the 'lateral margins' in opposite directions." Another group of aviation pioneers, financed by Alexander Graham Bell, "knew about the Wright patent but apparently had reservations about the wing-warping method .... Bell suggested wing flaps, or 'ailerons,' which had been used in France. [Glenn] Curtiss subsequently incorporated this concept in his successful flights of 1908 .... The Wrights sued Curtiss for patent infringement in 1909, claiming that their method applied to wing flaps as well as wing twisting. After protracted litigation, Orville Wright, ..., won the case in 1914 .... Curtiss [then made] a small change in his method of controlling the ailerons, which required the Wright corporation to begin litigating anew. Orville Wright sold out at this point, but the successor company continued to press its claims. With the formal entry of the United States into World War I imminent, however, a solution to the patent litigation was sought by the government since some firms were reluctant to take contracts because of the threat of patent infringement suits. The Wright-Martin Company ... was threatening to sue those considered to be infringers—effectively any airplane manufacturer" (George Bittlingmayer, "Property Rights, Progress, and the Aircraft Patent Agreement," *Journal of Law and Economics*, 31 [April 1988]: 230-32). As the author of this study points out in a footnote: "It seems unlikely that broad definitions—a patent on the automobile or on the airplane—could be defended on economic grounds. Although the Wright brothers threw their energies into airplane invention in the hope of becoming wealthy ... others, imagining much smaller rewards looming ahead of them, were right behind. The development of a successful flying machine was only a matter of time, and it is unlikely that the introduction of the airplane a few years sooner would have been worth a monopoly grant on the airplane ..." (p. 246n).

[21]" ... for nearly a quarter of a century, for example, James Watt was able to prevent other engineers from constructing new types of steam engine, even under license from himself" (Ashton, *The Industrial Revolution*, p. 10). At least one

technology": In October 1992, the U.S. Patent and Trademarks Office awarded to a single company, Agracetus Inc., of Middleton, Wisconsin, a patent for rights to *all forms* of genetically engineered cotton—no matter what techniques or genes are used to create them—prompting the following comment from an executive in this industry: "It was as if the inventor of the assembly line had won property rights to all mass-produced goods, from automobiles to washing machines."[22]

(2) The existence of patents also induces wasteful expenditure of resources by competitors in order to "invent around the patent," i.e., develop competing products that are sufficiently differentiated so as not to infringe an existing patent. Nelson puts it this way: "There are incentives for a firm to duplicate the prevailing best technology patented by another firm in a way that does not infringe on patents. More generally, there are incentives for a firm to develop a technology even if it is worse than the current best one, if it is better than the one it has and the best is blocked by patents ...."[23] As Nelson points out, though these activities increase the level of "research and development" spending, from the social point of view they are not necessarily an efficient use of available resources.[24]

---

historian argues that the Industrial Revolution did not really take off until 1785, the year Watt's patent expired (Louis Rougier, *The Genius of the West* [Los Angeles: Nash Publishing Co., 1971], p. 118).

[22]Richard Stone, "Intellectual Property: Sweeping Patents Put Biotech Companies on the Warpath," *Science*, 268 (5 May 1995): 656.

[23]Richard R. Nelson, "Assessing Private Enterprise: An Exegesis of Tangled Doctrine," *Bell Journal of Economics*, 12 (Spring 1981): 107; see also, by the same author, "Research on Productivity Growth and Productivity Differences: Dead Ends and New Departures," *Journal of Economic Literature*, 19 (Sept 1981): 1047.

[24]Worse still, patent-owners also have incentives to do the same thing (i.e., "invent around" their own patents) in order to preclude potential competition. To the extent that these activities are induced by the patent system itself, resources devoted to them (as well as the associated legal expenses) are essentially wasted from the social point of view, and should be regarded as another cost of the system. To cite an example, Bresnahan mentions that, to protect its monopoly position in the market for plain-paper copiers, Xerox patented every conceivable aspect of its technology. "IBM had spent millions to 'invent around' Xerox's

(3) Technological innovation is often stimulated precisely when patents are not very effective. This was the case of the Eastman Kodak company, that decided to adopt its well-known policy of permanent research and "continuous innovation" as a way to maintain its competitive leadership in view of the practical impossibility of enforcing all its patents.[25] Presumably, had they been able to enforce their patents they might well have devoted fewer resources for research and development of new products, and technological development in this industry would have been less rapid.

(4) An aspect of the problem that does not always receive enough consideration is that the existence of patents might distort incentives, diverting inventive activity towards more easily "patentable" products. Again, we should bear in mind that not all discoveries and innovations are patentable, even when they are highly beneficial. Milton Friedman made a very interesting comment in this regard in his book, *Capitalism and Freedom* (1962). After declaring himself in favor of patents, he added: "At the same time, there are costs involved. For one thing, there are many 'inventions' that are not patentable. The 'inventor' of the supermarket, for example, conferred great benefits on his fellowmen for which he could not charge them. Insofar as the same kind of ability is required for the one kind of invention as for the other, the existence of patents tends to divert activity to patentable inventions."[26] The 64 dollar question: Would we really have fewer

---

major patents—with 25 percent of the budget going for patent counsel, not R&D" (Timothy F. Bresnahan, "Post-Entry Competition in the Plain Paper Copier Market," *American Economic Review*, 75 [May 1985]: 16). For an interesting case-study of "preemptive patenting" during the early history of radio broadcasting see Leonard S. Reich, "Research, Patents, and the Struggle to Control Radio," *Business History Review*, 51 (Summer 1977): 208-35.

[25]Reese V. Jenkins, "George Eastman and the Coming of Industrial Research in America," in C. W. Pursell (ed.), *Technology in America* (Cambridge: MIT Press, 1990), pp. 134-36.

[26]Milton Friedman, *Capitalism and Freedom* (Chicago: University of Chicago Press, 1962), p. 127. A case in point: "The biotech firm Genetics Institute decides which version of a drug to develop partly based on which iteration shows the best results in clinical trials but also according to which version can command the strongest patent protection. Genetics Institute patent counsel says the strength of the potential patent position is 'a leading factor' in deciding what research to pursue" (Rivette and Kline, *op cit.*, p. 58).

inventions in the absence of patent laws, or would we simply have different *kinds* of inventions?

5. The Case of Copyrights.[27]

Though they have had different legislative histories, patents and copyrights share many common features, and much of what has been said about patents applies equally well to copyrights.[28] Just as the pro-patents

---

[27]The views expressed in this section are largely based on Arnold Plant, "The Economic Aspects of Copyright in Books," in *Selected Economic Essays and Addresses* (London: Routledge & Kegan Paul, 1974), pp. 57-86, and Robert M. Hurt, "The Economic Rationale of Copyright," *American Economic Review*, 56 (May 1966): 421-32.

[28]Murray Rothbard thought that patents and copyrights are actually quite different forms of legal protection, and made a strong case *against* patents but *in favor* of copyrights (*Man, Economy and State* [Princeton: Van Nostrand, 1962], pp. 652-60). This is not a common viewpoint—opinions on intellectual property tend to be "all or nothing"—though it is a respectable position, and has a distinguished intellectual ancestry that can be traced at least as far back as Henry George: "The two things [patents and copyrights] are not alike, but essentially different. The copyright is not a right to the exclusive use of a fact, an idea, or a combination, which by the natural law of property all are free to use; but only to the labor expended in the thing itself. It does not prevent anyone from using for himself the facts, the knowledge, the laws or combinations for a similar production, but only from using the identical form of the particular book or other production—the actual labor which has in short been expended in producing it. It rests therefore upon the natural, moral right of each one to enjoy the products of his own exertion, and involves no interference with the similar right of anyone else to do likewise. The patent, on the other hand, prohibits any one from doing a similar thing, and involves, usually for a specified time, an interference with the equal liberty on which the right of ownership rests. The copyright is therefore in accordance with the moral law—it gives to the man who has expended the intangible labor required to write a particular book or paint a picture security against the copying of that identical thing. The patent is in defiance of this natural right. It prohibits others from doing what has already been attempted. Everyone has a moral right to think what I think, or to perceive what I perceive, or to do what I do—no matter whether he gets the hint from me or independently of me. Discovery can give no right of ownership, for whatever is discovered must have been already here to be discovered. If a man makes a wheelbarrow, or a book, or a picture, he has a moral right to that particular wheelbarrow, or book, or picture, but no right to ask that others be prevented from making similar things. Such a prohibition, though given for the purpose of stimulating discovery and invention, really in the long run

literature stresses inventors' rights, the pro-copyrights literature stresses the rights of authors and other creators to benefit from their creations, though it should be noted that the term "copyright," as currently used, actually comprises a bundle of several different rights that are unfortunately (and misleadingly) conflated due to the use of a single concept to cover the whole bundle.

The expressions used in other languages to denote "copyright" (*derecho de autor, droit d'auter, diritto d'autore, direito do autor*) literally translate as "authors' rights," which includes the notion of copyright in the narrower sense (the right to control reproduction of the work), though it also implies that a broader range of different rights are also intended. These include the so-called "moral rights" of the author, which view literary and artistic works as extensions of the author's personality, and encompass the following protections: (1) the right to be identified as the creator of the work (so-called "paternity rights" of authorship and protections against plagiarism), and (2) protections against unauthorized alterations or mutilations of the work (so-called "integrity rights" of authorship). As opposed to mere copyright, these two moral rights of authorship have always been regarded as inalienable and perpetual. A third moral right is also recognized: the right to withhold publication, which is an aspect of a broader right to privacy, although it is not always clear whether it should be regarded as perpetual or whether it applies only to living authors (i.e., if society should be bound by an author's wishes after his death.)

Opposition to copyright in the narrower sense obviously does not imply opposition to the moral rights of authorship, which are very ancient legal concepts. Copyright, on the other hand, is a fairly recent notion, which dates from about the time of the invention of printing. Whether or not we regard the right to control the reproduction of creative works as a "natural right" of authors, the historical fact is that prior to the invention of printing this right was not regarded as implicit in the concept of authorship. Copyright law was created by specific acts of legislation, and every extension of its scope to cover new productions resulting from

---

operates as a check upon them"—*Progress and Poverty* [1879] (New York: Robert Schalkenbach Foundation, 1990), p. 411 (footnote). It is interesting to note that, once we establish a major distinction between copyrights and patents, four situations are theoretically possible: one might favor both (the conventional view), one might oppose both (a minority view), one might favor copyright but oppose patents (the George-Rothbard view), or one might oppose copyright but favor patents (a conceptual possibility, though it appears to be an empty set—no one seems to have articulated this position publicly).

technological innovations (such as photography, phonographic recordings of musical creations, film productions, computer software) has required special legislation to that effect, since these extensions did not arise "naturally" from judicial decisions, as the courts were unwilling to apply to these situations a concept created specifically for the case of printed books:

> The concept of copyright is rooted in the technology of print. The recognition of a copyright and the practice of paying royalties emerged with the printing press .... Copyright was a specific adaptation to a specific technology, and to the problems and opportunities it created. The law recognized that. The landmark case in the United States was *White Smith v. Apollo* [1908]. It denied protection to piano rolls or sound recordings because they were not "writings" in tangible form readable by a human being. That common law concept of copyright excluded from protection many new technologies of communication since 1908. But the motion picture industry, the recording industry, and more recently the broadcasting industry have persuaded Congress to extend various protections to them, since courts were not willing to do so .... However, with the arrival of radio and electronic reproduction, and now photocopy reproduction, the concept becomes inappropriate. There is no easy way to keep tabs on the numerous reproductions in somewhat variable form that can take place in innumerable locations with these new technologies. The analogy is to word-of-mouth communications in the 18th century, not to the print shop of that period. Nonetheless, information and publishing industries whose welfare and survival depends on finding some way to charge for their information processing services have latched on to copyright protection under statute law, and are trying to get the courts or the Congress to extend copyright protection to computerized data, photocopies, and telereproduction. Though recognizing that in those technologies the existent copyright law is basically unenforceable, they nonetheless grab on to whatever frail reed it may provide rather than turn to the even frailer reed of trying to invent, and to get into legislation, some entirely new as yet undevised system for rewarding the creators of information .... the U. S. Congress passed a new copyright law in 1976, which was designed to solve all the new problems of copyright for cable television, photocopying, and computers. It has solved few if any of them .... How inappropriate the concept of copyright is to computer communications becomes evident as we examine how the law has to squirm to deal with the simplest problems .... the process of computer communication entails processing of texts that are partly controlled by people and partly automatic. They are happening all over the system. Some of the text is never visible but is only stored electronically: some is flashed briefly on a terminal display; some is printed out in hard copy .... The receivers may be individuals and clearly identified, or they may be

passers-by with access but whose access is never recorded; the passer-by may only look, as a reader browsing through a book, or he may make an automatic copy; sometimes the program will record that, sometimes it will not. To try to apply the concept of copyright to all these stages and actors would require a most elaborate set of regulations. It has none of the simplicity of checking what copies rolled off a printing press .... One would like to compensate an author if a computer terminal is used as a printing press to run off numerous copies of a valuable text. One would not like to impose any control as someone works at a terminal in the role of a reader and checks back and forth through various files. The boundary, however, is impossible to draw. In the new technology of interactive computing the reader, the writer, the bookseller, and the printer have become one. In the old technology of printing one could have a right to free press for the reader and the writer but try to enforce copyright on the printer and the bookseller. That distinction will no longer work, any more than it would ever have worked in the past on conversation. Those whose livelihood is at stake in copyright do not like that kind of comment. They contend that creative work must be compensated. Indeed, it must .... But the system must be practical to work .... in an era of infinitely varied, automated text manipulation there is no reasonable way to count copies and charge royalties on them .... It may be very unfair to authors. It may have a profoundly negative effect on some aspects of culture, and in any case, whether positive or negative, it may change things considerably. If it becomes more difficult for authors and artists to be paid by a royalty scheme, more of them will seek salaried bases from which to work. Some may try to get paid by personal appearances or other auxiliaries to fame. Or the highly illustrated, well-bound book may acquire a special significance if the mere words of the text are hard to protect. Or one may try to sell subscriptions to a continuing service, ... These are the kinds of considerations one must think about in speculating about the consequences for culture of a world where the royalty-carrying unit copy is no longer easy to protect in many of the domains where it has been dominant .... it is clear that with photocopiers and computers, copyright is an anachronism. Like many other unenforceable laws that we keep on the statute books from the past, this one may be with us for some time to come, but with less and less effect.[29]

The final passages from this rather long quotation suggest the intriguing possibility that, in arguing whether authors "should" have a copyright over their creations, we may be posing what will increasingly become a "moot" question: Technological developments in certain

---

[29]Ithiel de Sola Pool, *Technologies without Boundaries: On Telecommunications in a Global Age* (Cambridge: Harvard University Press, 1990), pp. 254-59.

areas—photocopiers, video and sound recording, computer scanning, etc.—are making it harder and harder to enforce the laws. At some point, we might just have to give up (we may have already reached this point in the case of musical recordings, due to the development of downloadable ".mp3" computer files[30]), so the interesting question then becomes: What would be the consequences of a world without copyright? Since the main *utilitarian* argument for copyright is that it stimulates literary and artistic creation, the relevant question should be: Would the absence of copyright significantly affect the quality and quantity of literary/artistic output?

1) Even today, most authors never make much money writing books, and some actually print their works with their own money. Others are willing to accept payment in copies of their works (often in the form of off-prints of journal articles). Much scientific and academic writing is of this kind. For many of these authors, writing for publication is a way to increase their "brand-name capital" in order to obtain higher incomes from other activities. Other authors are interested in spreading their views, so they would presumably have no interest in discouraging reproduction of their writings—provided their authorship is acknowledged, they would be quite happy if others were willing to reprint them with their own resources. The output of this type of writing would evidently not be much affected by the absence of copyright.

2) A second type of writer does it for a living. If there is no other way to reward them, then the absence of copyright would most likely reduce total literary output. The question is whether copyright is the only way to guarantee an income for this type of writer. Plant thought that writers would find a way to sell their product, provided that a demand for it exists at all—note that copyright does not *create* this demand, it only provides a means to *monopolize* a demand once it exists.[31] We cannot know *a priori* what kinds of market structures would dominate in a different legal setting, though possibly (as suggested by Pool) there would be greater reliance on salaried writers for subscription-type publications, perhaps with content more or less "given away" as

---

[30]For a balanced and very informative analysis of the implications of the "mp3" revolution see Charles C. Mann, "The Heavenly Jukebox," *Atlantic Monthly*, 286 (Sept 2000): 39-59.

[31]Plant, "The Economic Aspects of Copyright in Books," p. 61.

loss-leaders in order to stimulate sales of other products.[32] Also, as Pool suggested, there might be greater reliance on collateral sources of income, such as personal appearances, lectures, consulting, live performances,[33] etc. Whether alternative market arrangements would fully compensate the loss of income currently derived from copyright is an empirical question. Best-selling writers and composers might very well earn less money in a world without copyright. If so, then the *quantity* of literary and artistic output would most likely be lower. How much lower we cannot know.

3) A very ingenious argument proposed by Plant suggests that in the case of book publishing, it is likely that the absence of copyright protection would result in a smaller number of *titles* published.[34] This would not necessarily be a bad thing, since what we really want is not more titles, but more good books at lower prices. Plant argues that the copyright system has a somewhat perverse consequence, in that it encourages publication of a broader range of titles, but not enough copies of the books people really want to read. Due to the nature of his business, a publisher cannot be sure of the success of a new title, and most titles

---

[32]This is the business model underlying present-day journalism, which essentially hires staff-writers in order to help sell the main product, which is advertising. There are many other examples of this type of arrangement. For instance, early radio broadcasters were subsidized by radio manufacturers, who were willing to lose money on broadcasting in order to stimulate demand for radio sets. Incidentally, it seems to me this is probably how the market would solve the problem of computer software in the absence of copyright. It is often claimed that if software could be copied freely, then software developers would have no incentive to create it. Note, however, that *hardware* manufacturers would have an incentive to support software development (and perhaps even give it away for free), since the availability of more and better software increases the demand for hardware.

[33]In the case of music, it is interesting to note that, prior to the development of the phonograph, copyright over music applied only to sheet music, i.e., it did not extend to the musical performance. It is an open question whether the gradual extension of copyright to cover not only musical recordings but *any* kind of public performance has resulted in increased quantity and quality of musical composition. In any case, if musical recordings could be freely copied (which in practice increasingly happens to be the case now), musicians would still have an incentive to compose and record music in order to stimulate the demand for live performances.

[34]Plant, *op. cit.*, pp. 72, 80.

in fact do not cover costs. However, when a title is successful it can be quite profitable, and these profits subsidize losses from unsuccessful titles. Since a publisher cannot know beforehand which new titles will be the successful ones, publishing has some aspects of a lottery: In order to make money on the successful titles, the publisher has to take a chance on many different titles, most of which he knows will be failures. Copyright affects this situation by increasing the profitability of successful titles: In terms of the lottery, copyright protection increases the "prize" without affecting, on the other hand, the risks involved. *Ceteris paribus*, we expect that, with equal risks, a larger prize will induce a player to buy more "tickets." Therefore, more *titles* will be published under a copyright system, but the resulting monopoly position guarantees that the books people really want (the successful titles) will be published in smaller quantities and at higher prices.

5. Conclusions.

Issues related to intellectual property rights are becoming increasingly important in policy discussions. Technological developments have created whole new areas of patentable products that pose problems for the definition and delimitation of "property rights"—e.g., computer software and bio-technologies, to mention only two of the most noteworthy areas at the cutting edge of leading technologies (witness the problems involved in "patenting life-forms,"[35] and the question of so-called "internet patents"[36]). At the same time, some of these very developments are making it harder to enforce many of the more conventional forms of intellectual property—the advent of ".mp3" file-swapping on the Internet, for instance, which raises questions regarding the future viability of copyright in musical recordings. The strains and stresses which the newer technologies are imposing on current intellectual property law are resulting in calls for tougher and more stringent enforcement of existing

---

[35]See John H. Barton, "Patenting Life," *Scientific American*, 264 (March 1991): 18-24.

[36]In October 1999 Priceline.com sued Microsoft's Expedia group for infringement of its patented "name your own price" auction system, while Amazon.com, the leading Internet book retailer, sued its main rival, Barnes & Noble, for infringement of its patented "one-click" ordering system (Rivette and Kline, "Discovering New Value in Intellectual Property," pp. 56, 66).

legal mechanisms. The United States government has for several years taken the lead worldwide in pressuring other countries to strengthen their intellectual property laws and make them conform more closely to current U. S. standards.

In view of developments such as these, now is as good a time as any for a radical rethinking of traditional intellectual property concepts. Perhaps, instead of considering reforms to *strengthen* patents and copyrights, we should be moving in the opposite direction? To be sure, given current trends, copyright might well die out on its own, whether we like it or not. If so, discussions of the merits of copyright will become essentially "moot" questions. As for patents, in the absence of precise estimates of the costs and benefits of patent systems, we cannot provide an unequivocal answer to the question posed in the title. Perhaps we will never know for sure. However, we *can* point out that the benefits stressed by the pro-patents camp turn out, on closer inspection, to be smaller than is conventionally assumed, while there are many costs involved that can easily be overlooked. The cost/benefit relationship is thus not as favorable as the pro-patent camp would have us believe. At the very least, we should oppose current efforts to broaden the scope of patent and copyright laws until a stronger case can be made that the benefits do indeed exceed the costs.

BIBLIOGRAPHY

Ashton, T. S. *The Industrial Revolution, 1760-1830*. Oxford University Press, 1964 [1948].

Barlow, John Perry. "Selling Wine without Bottles: The Economy of Mind on the Global Net", in Peter Ludlow (ed.), *High Noon on the Electronic Frontier: Conceptual Issues in Cyberspace*, pp. 9-34. Cambridge, MA: MIT Press, 1996. [Originally published as "The Economy of Ideas: A Framework for Patents and Copyrights in the Digital Age (Everything You Know about Intellectual Property is Wrong)", *Wired*, 2.03 (1994): 85-90, 126-29.]

Barton, John H. "Patenting Life." *Scientific American*, 264 (March 1991): 18-24.

Bittlingmayer, George. "Property Rights, Progress, and the Aircraft Patent Agreement." *Journal of Law and Economics*, 31 (April 1988): 227-48.

Bresnahan, Timothy F. "Post-Entry Competition in the Plain Paper Copier Market." *American Economic Review*, 75 (May 1985): 15-19.

Coase, R. H. "Professor Sir Arnold Plant: His Ideas and Influence," in M. J. Anderson (ed.), *The Unfinished Agenda: Essays on the Political Economy of Government Policy in Honour of Arthur Seldon*, pp. 81-90. London: Institute of Economic Affairs, 1986.

Denison, Edward F. *Accounting for Slower Economic Growth*. Washington: Brookings Institution, 1979.

Desrochers, Pierre. "On the Abuse of Patents as Economic Indicators." *Quarterly Journal of Austrian Economics*, 1 (Winter 1998): 51-74.

Flink, James J. "Henry Ford and the Triumph of the Automobile," in C. W. Pursell (ed.), *Technology in America*, pp. 177-89. Cambridge: MIT Press, 1990.

Franklin, Benjamin. *The Autobiography of Benjamin Franklin*, Harvard Classics, vol. 1. New York: P. F. Collier & Son, 1909.

Friedman, Milton. *Capitalism and Freedom*. University of Chicago Press, 1962.

George, Henry. *Progress and Poverty* [1879]. New York: Robert Schalkenbach Foundation, 1990.

Griliches, Zvi. "Patent Statistics as Economic Indicators: A Survey." *Journal of Economic Literature*, 28 (1990): 1661-1707.

Hayek, F. A. " 'Free' Enterprise and Competitive Order" [1947], in *Individualism and Economic Order*, pp. 107-18. University of Chicago Press, 1948.

————. *The Fatal Conceit.* University of Chicago Press, 1988.

Hurt, Robert M. "The Economic Rationale of Copyright." *American Economic Review*, 56 (May 1966): 421-32.

Jefferson, Thomas. "Letter to Isaac McPherson (August 13, 1813)," in Merrill D. Peterson (ed.), *The Portable Thomas Jefferson*. New York: Viking Press, 1975.

Jenkins, Reese V. "George Eastman and the Coming of Industrial Research in America," in C. W. Pursell (ed.), *Technology in America*, pp. 129-41. Cambridge: MIT Press, 1990.

Kinsella, N. Stephan. "Against Intellectual Property." *Journal of Libertarian Studies*, 15 (Spring 2001): 1-54.

Machlup, Fritz and Edith T. Penrose. "The Patent Controversy in the Nineteenth Century." *Journal of Economic History*, 10 (May 1950): 1-29.

Mann, Charles C. "The Heavenly Jukebox." *Atlantic Monthly*, 286 (Sept 2000): 39-59.

Mansfield, Edwin, Mark Schwartz and Samuel Wagner. "Imitation Costs and Patents: An Empirical Study." *Economic Journal*, 91 (Dec 1981): 907-18.

Mansfield, Edwin. "The R&D Tax Credit and Other Technology Policy Issues." *American Economic Review*, 76 (May 1986): 190-94.

Meier, Hugo A. "Thomas Jefferson and a Democratic Technology," in C. W. Pursell (ed.), *Technology in America*, pp. 17-33. Cambridge: MIT Press, 1990.

Mokyr, Joel. *The Lever of Riches: Technological Creativity and Economic*

Progress. Oxford University Press, 1990.

Nelson, Richard R. "Assessing Private Enterprise: An Exegesis of Tangled Doctrine." *Bell Journal of Economics*, 12 (Spring 1981): 93-111.

—————. "Research on Productivity Growth and Productivity Differences: Dead Ends and New Departures." *Journal of Economic Literature*, 19 (Sept 1981): 1029-64.

North, Douglass C. "Sources of Productivity Change in Ocean Shipping, 1600-1850." *Journal of Political Economy*, 76 (Sept/Oct 1968): 953-70.

—————. *Structure and Change in Economic History.* New York: Norton, 1981.

Novak, Michael. *The Fire of Invention.* Lanham, Maryland: Rowman & Littlefield, 1997.

Palmer, Tom G. "Intellectual Property: A Non-Posnerian Law and Economics Approach." *Hamline Law Review*, 12 (Spring 1989): 261-304.

—————. "Are Patents and Copyrights Morally Justified?" *Harvard Journal of Law and Public Policy*, 13 (Summer 1990): 817-65.

Plant, [Sir] Arnold. "The Economic Theory Concerning Patents for Inventions" [1934], in *Selected Economic Essays and Addresses*, pp. 35-56. London: Routledge & Kegan Paul, 1974.

—————. "The Economic Aspects of Copyright in Books" [1934], in *Selected Economic Essays and Addresses*, pp. 57-86. London: Routledge & Kegan Paul, 1974.

Pool, Ithiel de Sola. *Technologies without Boundaries: On Telecommunications in a Global Age.* Cambridge: Harvard University Press, 1990.

Reich, Leonard S. "Research, Patents, and the Struggle to Control Radio." *Business History Review*, 51 (Summer 1977): 208-35.

Rivette, Kevin G., and David Kline. "Discovering New Value in Intellectual Property." *Harvard Business Review*, 78 (Jan-Feb 2000): 54-66.

Rothbard, Murray N. *Man, Economy and State: A Treatise on Economic Principles.* Princeton: Van Nostrand, 1962.

Rougier, Louis. *The Genius of the West.* Los Angeles: Nash Publishing Co., 1971.

Sakakibara, Mariko and Lee Branstetter. "Do Stronger Patents Induce More Innovation? Evidence from the 1988 Japanese Patent Law Reforms." Working Paper 7066, National Bureau of Economic Research, April 1999.

Scherer, F. M. "Nordhaus' Theory of Optimal Patent Life: A Geometric Interpretation." *American Economic Review,* 62 (June 1972): 422-27.

Sherwood, Robert M. *Intellectual Property and Economic Development.* Boulder: Westview Press, 1990.

Solow, Robert M. "Technical Change and the Aggregate Production Function." *Review of Economics and Statistics*, 39 (1957): 312-20.

Stone, Richard. "Intellectual Property: Sweeping Patents Put Biotech Companies on the Warpath." *Science*, 268 (5 May 1995): 656-58.

Timberg, Sigmund. "The Effect of the European Common Market on Anti-Trust and Patent Policy," in Crawford Shaw (ed.), *Legal Problems in International Trade and Investment,* pp. 71-88. New Haven: Yale Law School, 1962.

Addendum[1]

The Global Governance of Knowledge: Patent Offices and their Clients,
by Peter Drahos.

Cambridge University Press, 2010, xv + 351 pp., £25.99.

"Patent office administration would strike many a person as a dull topic"
(p. xiv). This seems like an inauspicious opening sentence for a book on
patent office administration, and the author is of course quite right. It is
not a very exciting subject.

It is an *important* subject, nonetheless, and Peter Drahos does a very
good job of explaining what it is, exactly, that these bureaucracies do, how
they go about their day-to-day routines, and who their major clients are.
Moreover, he describes how the different national patent offices have
gradually become part of a globally integrated international patent system
that, he argues, serves in practice to protect the interests of large
multinational corporations. Given the strong monopoly provisions of the
patent system, this is a matter of central importance that touches all aspects
of business innovation.

Drahos states that he began his study with the hypothesis that "patent
offices around the world are cooperating to integrate their administrative
procedures and technical systems," thereby building a system for what he
calls the "global governance of knowledge" (p. 3). To investigate this
hypothesis, he gathered information about the extent of cooperation
among the different national patent offices. His main source of information
was a series of interviews conducted over a five-year period (2004 to
2008), in the course of which he interviewed 140 officials from 45
different patent offices, ranging from the largest and most important—the
US Patent and Trademark Office (USPTO), the European Patent Office
(EPO), the Japanese Patent Office (JPO), the so-called "Trilaterals"—to
some of the smallest patent offices in the world.

One main finding is that, although patent law in theory continues to be
an area over which countries have sovereign discretion, in practice "[t]he
network of patent offices is not a flat structure of equals. Rather it is a
tiered structure dominated by a core of large offices made up of the EPO,
JPO and the USTPO ...." (p. 46).

---

[1]This review was published originally in *Prometheus*, 29 (1) (2011): 51-54.

> The patent offices outside of the core forge relationships with those in the core in different ways, but ... it is the core that leads when it comes to developing a global system of patent administration .... Developing-country offices ... are being encouraged to accept the standards and decisions of the core offices. Progressively an automation of decision-making is taking place in which independent examination by many offices will be replaced by examination by a very few and mechanical acceptance by the many (pp. 46-47).

Throughout the book, Drahos argues that a common culture is being developed, much of it the result of training programs for patent examiners and other forms of technical cooperation that the large core offices provide for developing country offices: "Much of the training that the Trilaterals provide for examiners in developing-country patent offices is aimed at building a borderless interpretive community when it comes to the application of now largely globalized patent law principles" (p. 53).

This is an arresting thesis, and much of the book is devoted to documenting it. Chapter 2 starts out by describing the essentials of patent office procedure, filing routes for patent applications, and grant procedures. The general sense is that patent law, in its practical application, is a game for insiders with rules designed for maximal complexity, and Drahos captures this quite well:

> The comparative advantage of patent attorneys lies not in their knowledge of patent law, but in their knowledge of many hundreds of rules and guidelines that make up patent procedure and the drafting of the claims that define an invention. A key part of their work is keeping track of the many deadlines that exist for the submission of documentation that accompanies the application process (p. 55).

"Welcome to the maze," as he puts it.

Chapter 3 provides a brief history of patent law and patent offices, and Chapters 4 to 10 are then devoted to descriptions of the characteristics and special problems of individual patent offices or groups of offices. Perhaps inevitably, the book loses much of its momentum in these sections, although we are often rewarded with interesting bits of information. One historical trend that comes across crystal clear is the tremendous growth in patenting activity. The USPTO, the largest and oldest patent office in the world, is the best example of this trend: 10,000 patents were granted in the United States from 1790 to 1836, an amount that by the 1920s was being granted every three months, and by 2006 the USPTO was receiving more than 417,000 patent applications per year (pp. 151-152). And that is just in the United States. Elsewhere, we are told that "collectively in 2007 the Trilaterals received a little over 993,000 applications" (p. 74).

One might naively assume that this should be a cause for rejoicing. All those new inventions! Those who know a little about the patent system are aware, however, that the rising flood of patents is not really a reflection of greater inventive activity. Rather, what it reflects is an increase in patenting *per se*. Drahos attributes this to a historical decline in the cost of patent office fees, plus what he describes as "the missionary behavior of the patent profession" (p. 109). At one point he compares patenting activity to an arms race, with patent offices and patent attorneys in the role of arms dealers:

> In an arms race one party tries to stay ahead of the other through stockpiling more arms in order to maintain superiority. The other party does precisely the same …. If some companies begin obtaining monopoly privileges their competitors are likely to follow suit. Naturally the attorneys and patent offices will encourage the purchase of more arms. If the costs of patenting are cheap one would expect patenting to go up. This of course means that patent offices will become flooded with patent applications (p. 109).

The result is administrative overload and overworked patent examiners under great pressure to reduce the growing backlog of pending applications by increasing their "productivity" by devoting less and less time to each individual patent application. One interesting statistic that emerges is that, among the Trilaterals, "time spent on the examination of an application generally falls into a range of 10 to 20 hours" (p. 74). This leads to the approval of many applications that would not survive a more rigorous scrutiny. Add to this another source of built-in bias, which comes from the nature of the patent office's business model. Patent offices depend upon their fee income, and most of that comes from renewal fees, a source of income that would dry up if the rejection rate for patent applications were too high:

> … under this kind of model [patent offices] have to ensure that a significant number of patent applications make it to grant, otherwise there will not be enough of a renewal stream of income …. If they issue a small number of patents, using, for example, a much more stringent test of inventiveness, they will have to contend with a lower income (pp. 19-20).

And herein lies the danger of the *de facto* harmonization of patent systems that Drahos sees as emerging via the "interpretive community" that he describes throughout the book: "In the case of patents there is a potential cost if the developing-country patent examiner is automatically following the low-quality output of developed-country examiners" (p. 262).

A related consequence of this business model is that patent offices have gradually developed a client-orientation and a "customer focus," much like private businesses. The problem, however, is that the "client" in this scenario is not the general public, but the giant corporations who are by far the largest users of the patent system. Ideally, patent offices have a public mission, and Drahos repeatedly refers to what he calls the "patent social contract," namely, the idea that society is willing to grant monopolies to inventors in exchange for the production of non-obvious and socially useful inventions. This notion underlies (and justifies) all existing patent laws. In practice, however, this is not how patent officials view their mission. Indeed, Drahos reports that in more than 140 interviews, this idea of a patent social contract was only mentioned twice (p. 38). Rather than being beholden to the public interest, "[a]n organization that operates on a fee-for-service basis is likely to see the person paying the fee as its customer" (p. 159). In the case of patent offices, "the persons paying the fees" are increasingly the large multinational corporations, and if they had their way they would patent everything under the sun. However, as Drahos points out:

> The patent social contract is not a contract aimed at the grant of more and more patents, but rather at the diffusion of more and more significant inventions .... citizens acting rationally would only want to grant monopoly rewards to inventions that were genuinely creative .... It is high-quality inventions that society wants, not high-quality patents which can only be a means to an end and never an end in themselves (pp. 78-79).

This is as good a statement as any of what we might call the "conventional view" on the relationship between patents and inventive activity. Defenders of the patent system never cease to stress the need to stimulate further technological development, and the implicit assumption is that patents are in fact the cause (or at least one important cause) of technical progress. This assumption has been so much taken for granted that evidence is hardly ever offered to support it. Moreover, when it *has* been examined empirically, the evidence almost uniformly fails to confirm it, and there is nothing in this book to suggest otherwise. On the other hand, Drahos provides ample support for the view that the patent system imposes large costs upon society, and that its main beneficiaries are (1) the large corporations that hold the vast majority of patents, and (2) their patent attorneys.[2] The "patent social contract" supposedly balances a social good

---

[2] A recent book by James Bessen and Michael J. Meurer, *Patent Failure: How*

(technical innovation) against a social bad (monopoly), though one should more properly speak of a presumed social good, since we cannot say for sure that patents do in fact significantly stimulate invention. Even Drahos is skeptical in this regard:

> Whether this staggering global growth in patent bureaucracy and patent regulation of markets actually caused much important scientific and technological innovation that would otherwise not have occurred, and at a cost that did not outweigh the benefits, is a question to which we will probably never have an answer (p. 285).

Monopoly, on the other hand, is unquestionably a social bad, and patents are nothing more than legal monopoly privileges granted by state *fiat*, which is why there has always been a dissenting tradition within economics that views patents with suspicion. Since the costs are obvious and the benefits doubtful at best, why not just do away with patents altogether?

Drahos does not draw this extreme conclusion, and instead he outlines in Chapter 11 a series of proposals designed to "reclaim the patent social contract." Space does not allow for a detailed discussion of these proposals. Suffice it to say that they are interesting and sensible, and I wish him well in his efforts in this regard. However, he will perhaps forgive me if, on the basis of the evidence that he himself amasses in this book, I also remain somewhat skeptical about the possibilities of actual implement-tation of his suggestions. In fact, it seems to me that this book identifies and describes important problems in the global patent system, without expressly drawing the conclusions that they warrant. There seems to be widespread agreement that today's patent system is broken, and although Drahos is among those who think it can still be fixed, some of us think it is broken beyond repair. We should consider the possibility that the patent system is simply unreformable.[3]

But an author is entitled to his own opinions. This is a very informative book, and I highly recommend it to anyone who is seriously interested in intellectual property issues. Drahos also writes well, and he even manages

---

Judges, Bureaucrats, and Lawyers Put Innovators at Risk (Princeton, NJ: University Press, 2008), suggests that the lion's share of those benefits actually accrue to the patent attorneys.

[3]For a spirited argument in favor of intellectual property "abolitionism" see Michele Boldrin and David K. Levine, *Against Intellectual Monopoly* (Cambridge: Cambridge University Press, 2008).

to inject occasional humor into this inherently dry subject. My personal favorite: "Patent harmonization negotiations become like a circus act in which the clowns go through a fixed routine while pretending spontaneity …. [They] are a circus, but without the laughs" (pp. 50-51).

IV. Studies on Milton Friedman

6

MILTON FRIEDMAN (1912-2006)[1]

"Let us now praise famous men, ..."
(Ecclesiasticus, 44:1)

Milton Friedman, who died in the early morning of November 16, 2006, was a world-famous economist, and an ardent and effective advocate of the free-market economy. Much of his celebrity derived from his role as public intellectual, an aspect of his work that was reflected largely in popular books, such as *Capitalism and Freedom* (1962) and the hugely successful *Free to Choose* (1980)—both co-authored with his wife, Rose (and the latter based on the television documentary of the same title)—and in the *Newsweek* opinion columns he wrote for many years.

Though he was already well-known by the time he received the Nobel Prize in Economics, in 1976, both his stature as public figure and his effectiveness as policy advocate were greatly enhanced by that award, and this is what has been mostly stressed in the vast outpouring of obituaries and public testimonials prompted by his recent passing.

It is important to recall, however, that there was another aspect of his career, one which most professional economists (and probably Friedman himself) would regard as far more important than his incursions in the policy arena. Indeed, even if "Friedman the public intellectual" had never existed, "Friedman the economic scientist" would still be renowned and respected (though perhaps not as a *bona fide* world-class celebrity), and his memory will live long in the lore of economics.

It is primarily this other aspect of his life and work that I wish to focus on in this essay.

---

[1]Published originally in *Independent Review*, 12 (1) (2007): 115-28.

1. Education and Professional Background.

Milton Friedman was born in Brooklyn, New York, on July 31, 1912, the youngest child in a family of poor Jewish immigrants from Carpatho-Ruthenia (then in the Hungarian part of Austria-Hungary, nowadays a part of independent Ukraine).

His early schooling was in the public school system of Rahway, New Jersey, were he grew up, and in 1928 he obtained a state scholarship to attend Rutgers University, which he entered with the intention of majoring in mathematics (his original career plan was to eventually become an actuary). In college, however, chance intervened, as he puts it, in the form of "two extraordinary teachers [of economics] who had a major impact on my life": Homer Jones and Arthur F. Burns (Friedman, 2004, p. 68). Under their influence, he switched majors from mathematics to economics.

Upon graduation from Rutgers in 1932, in the middle of the Great Depression, Friedman received two scholarship offers for graduate study, one to study economics at the University of Chicago, the other to study applied mathematics at Brown University. Both, it seems, were equally attractive: "It was close to a toss of a coin that determined which offer I accepted" (Friedman, 2004, p. 69). In the event, he opted for Chicago, and became an economist.[2]

At Chicago, where he earned his master's degree in 1933, his teachers included Frank Knight, Lloyd Mints, Henry Simons, Henry Schultz, and Jacob Viner.[3] There, he also met two fellow graduate students, W. Allen Wallis and George J. Stigler, who would become life-long friends and colleagues.[4] His friendship with Stigler was especially significant, as the Stigler-Friedman team, more than any other pairing of individuals, would

---

[2]Whether he would have had an equally illustrious career had he opted for mathematics at Brown is anybody's guess.

[3]Friedman had fond recollections of Viner— "[His] course was unquestion-ably the greatest intellectual experience of my life" (Friedman, 2004, p. 70)—and several generations of Viner's students have attested to his qualities as teacher, though he also seems to have been quite fearsome in class. Another great economist recalls: "I had the opportunity to take Jacob Viner's celebrated course in graduate economic theory—celebrated both for its profundity in analysis and history of thought, but also celebrated for Viner's ferocious manhandling of students, in which he not only reduced women to tears but on his good days drove returned paratroopers into hysteria and paralysis" (Samuelson, 1972, p. 161).

[4]Another classmate was Rose Director, his future wife and co-author. They were married on June 25, 1938.

eventually define and personify what came to be known as the "Chicago School" of economics.[5]

The following year he went to Columbia University, where he studied mathematical statistics under Harold Hotelling, and economics with Wesley C. Mitchell and John M. Clark. He later returned to Chicago as research assistant to Henry Schultz, who was then working on his massive study of empirical demand curves.[6] From 1937 to 1940 he worked on analysis of income-expenditure surveys at the National Bureau of Economic Research (NBER).

At this point it is perhaps useful to pause and reflect on this remarkable educational experience. Though it resulted from a seemingly fortuitous combination of circumstances, it would have been very hard to deliberately plan a program better suited to his future professional development. At the theoretical level, the Chicago influence was of course decisive, though one of the most important aspects of Friedman's approach to economic research—his careful and detailed analysis of empirical

---

[5]See Friedman's touching tribute to his friend and colleague (Friedman, 1999), and the recently published Friedman-Stigler correspondence (Hammond and Hammond, 2006). The "Chicago School" became a powerhouse in academic economics, and the University of Chicago's Department of Economics is, to date, the institution with the largest number of Nobel Prizes in Economics to its credit (see Rowley [1999] for profiles of five Chicago Nobelists).

[6]Schultz (1938). In the introduction to this volume, Schultz wrote the following: "In the fall of 1934, when I returned from a year's stay abroad and was faced with the prospect of having to train and build up an entirely new staff of assistants in order to finish the work, Milton Friedman, a former graduate student of mine, came to my rescue and for a year continued to render valuable assistance" (p. xi). A further, and more specific, acknowledgement is noted on p. 569 (note 1): "I am profoundly grateful to Mr. Milton Friedman for invaluable assistance in the preparation and writing of these chapters [i.e., Chapters 18 and 19] and for permission to summarize a part of his unpublished paper on indifference curves in Sec. III, chap. xix." The section Schultz was referring to is entitled "The Friedman Modification of the Johnson-Allen Definition of Complementarity," and is based on an unpublished paper by Friedman entitled "The Fitting of Indifference Curves as a Method of Deriving Statistical Demand Curves" (Jan 1934). This must have been Friedman's first technical paper in economics (note that he was 21 years old at the time!). It was never published, though it is occasionally cited in the literature on complementarity (see, for instance, Samuelson, 1974), and two Japanese scholars have recently developed some implications of Friedman's analysis (Tsujimura and Tsuzuki, 1998). (I would like to thank Mr. Takashi Yoshida, of Keio University, for kindly providing me a copy of the Tsujimura-Tsuzuki paper.)

evidence—did not come from Chicago, but from his contact with Wesley Mitchell and the NBER. In fact, though empirical research is now regarded as a hallmark of "Chicago" economics, this is at least partly due to the later influence of Friedman himself. In the 1930s, and with the somewhat marginal exceptions of Henry Schultz and Paul Douglas, at Chicago the emphasis was more on theory than on empirical analysis (Reder, 1982).

In the early stages of his career, however, the most important influence was that of Hotelling. Indeed, at first Friedman showed more signs of becoming an eminent statistician than a great economist. One of his first professional publications developed a non-parametric technique for the analysis of variance under certain conditions (Friedman, 1937). As in the case of most of his analytic contributions, the motivation for the "Friedman test" was to facilitate the solution of practical problems posed by data analysis (in this case, income and expenditure data).[7]

During World War II, and after a brief stint at the Treasury Department, Friedman was a member of the "Statistical Research Group" at Columbia, working on combat problems and quality inspection for war materials.[8] This group comprised a truly dazzling collection of brilliant statistical minds, and their joint efforts would result, *inter alia*, in the development of "sequential analysis," a very important advance in statistical theory. Essentially, Friedman, together with Allen Wallis and a Navy captain (Garret Schuyler), noticed that the conventional method of taking samples of a predetermined size was inefficient, since it did not take into account information generated by the sample process itself. The idea was later rigorously developed by Abraham Wald, who proved the basic theorem underlying sequential testing, which was quickly adopted and

---

[7]Though not much used by economists, it is widely used in other fields. Indeed, it has become so standard in the field of non-parametric statistics that it is often referred to as simply the "Friedman test," without further attribution, and thus most of the people who use it routinely are probably not aware that the creator of this useful test and the famous economist are in fact the same person. See, for instance, Gibbons (1976), pp. 310-17.

[8]On the history of the Columbia-SRG see Wallis (1980). See also Rees (1980), who provides a briefer discussion of the material covered by Wallis, but set in a somewhat broader context. Wallis reports some of the titles of the studies prepared by the SRG. One particular title is rather chilling: "Relative Effectiveness of Caliber 0.50, Caliber 0.60, and 20 mm Guns as Armament for Multiple Anti-Aircraft Machine Gun Turrets" (Aug 28, 1945). This report was written by Milton Friedman.

adapted as the standard method for inspection sampling.[9]

After the war, Friedman served briefly on the faculty of the University of Minnesota, and in 1946 he returned to the University of Chicago as professor in the Department of Economics, where he stayed until his retirement in 1977. The return to Chicago coincided with a major change in the focus of his research activity, which shifted away from pure statistics, and eventually centered almost entirely on economics.

He was back home.

2. The Methodology of Positive Economics.

Friedman had a profound impact on economic research during his lifetime, and his influence reached far beyond the particular fields he chose for his own research. Much of this influence was due to his opinions on methodological issues, which were clarified at an early stage of his career. A famous 1953 essay on "The Methodology of Positive Economics" is arguably his best-known work among professional economists, as well as one of the most controversial.

Friedman began his essay by distinguishing between *positive economics*, a "body of systematized knowledge concerning what is," and *normative economics*, "a body of systematized knowledge discussing criteria of what ought to be" (Friedman, 1953, p. 3; unless otherwise stated, all page references in parentheses in this section are to this work). Both disciplines are related, though the conclusions of positive economics are independent of ethical positions or normative judgments. The purpose of positive economics is to "provide a system of generalizations that can be used to make correct predictions about the consequences of any change in circumstances" (p. 4). Economic theories should be evaluated according to strictly empirical criteria: "Viewed as a body of substantive hypotheses,

---

[9]See Armitage (1968) for a brief introduction to the literature on sequential analysis. Stigler was also a member of the SRG, though not as long as Friedman (10 months and 31 months, respectively). Stigler's take on the experience is characteristic: "[The SRG] was a pioneer American branch of the new craft called operations research, which applied statistical and economic theory to combat problems and to wartime procurement .... Our group had illustrious successes, such as the invention by Wald of a new method of statistical analysis called sequential analysis. That method of quality inspection saved the economy more money per month in the purchase of rocket propellant than the entire wartime cost of our organization. My role in our work was so modest that my claim must be that I did not aid the enemy" (Stigler, 1988, pp. 61-62).

theory is to be judged by its predictive power for the class of phenomena which it is intended to 'explain.' Only factual evidence can show whether it is 'right' or 'wrong' or, better, tentatively 'accepted' as valid or 'rejected'" (p. 8). This is stressed repeatedly throughout the essay:

> ... the only relevant test of the *validity* of a hypothesis is comparison of its predictions with experience. The hypothesis is rejected if its predictions are contradicted ("frequently" or more often than predictions from an alternative hypothesis); it is accepted if its predictions are not contradicted; great confidence is attached to it if it has survived many opportunities for contradiction (pp. 8-9, italics in the original).

Using language that is nowadays associated with Karl Popper's philosophy of science (Popper, 1959 [1934]), Friedman added that "factual evidence can never 'prove' a hypothesis; it can only fail to disprove it, which is what we generally mean when we say, somewhat inexactly, that the hypothesis has been 'confirmed' by experience" (p. 9).[10]

To be sure, the nature of economic phenomena presents special difficulties, since it is usually impossible to perform controlled experiments, explicitly designed to eliminate complicating factors. Therefore, "we must rely on evidence cast up by the 'experiments' that happen to occur" (p. 10). Friedman held, however, that "the inability to conduct so-

---

[10]Friedman nowhere cites Popper in his essay, which at first glance might seem puzzling, given the similarity of their views in this regard. It seems, however, that by the time of his first meeting with Popper, Friedman had already developed his methodological notions independently: "Shortly after I had completed a first draft [of the 1953 essay], George Stigler and I had long discussions with Karl Popper in 1947 at the founding meeting of the Mont Pelerin Society. The part of those discussions that I remember best had to do with scientific methodology. Popper's book, *Logik der Forschung*, published in Vienna in 1934, had already become a classic analysis of the methodology of the physical sciences, but my German was too limited for me to have read it even though I may have known about its existence. It was not translated into English until 1959, ..., so these discussions at Mont Pelerin were my first exposure to his views. I found them highly compatible with the views that I had independently come to, though far more sophisticated and more fully developed" (Friedman and Friedman, 1998, p. 215). The Mont Pelerin Society is an international association of scholars, founded at a conference in 1947 organized by F. A. Hayek, and committed to the preservation and dissemination of the ideals of classical liberalism. (On the history of the Mont Pelerin Society see Hartwell [1995]. Incidentally, Friedman, at age 34, must have been one of the youngest of the thirty-nine founding members. Since he lived a very long life, it is likely then that he was the last surviving member of that original group.)

called 'controlled experiments' does not, ... , reflect a basic difference between the social and physical sciences both because it is not peculiar to the social sciences—witness astronomy—and because the distinction between a controlled experiment and uncontrolled experience is at best one of degree. No experiment can be completely controlled, and every experience is partly controlled in the sense that some disturbing influences are relatively constant in the course of it" (p. 10).

Furthermore, "evidence cast up by experience is abundant and frequently as conclusive as that from contrived experiments; thus the inability to conduct experiments is not a fundamental obstacle to testing hypotheses by the success of their predictions" (p. 10). On the other hand, such evidence is admittedly "far more difficult to interpret. It is frequently complex and always indirect and incomplete. Its collection is often arduous, and its interpretation requires subtle analysis and involved chains of reasoning, which seldom carry real conviction" (pp. 10-11). In short, the "crucial" experiment is seldom possible in economics, which hinders adequate hypothesis testing, though "this is much less significant than the difficulty it places in the way of achieving a reasonably prompt and wide consensus on the conclusions justified by the available evidence" (p. 11). The process of weeding-out failed hypotheses is slower than in other sciences. On occasions, however, casual experience provides evidence that is just as dramatic as any controlled experiment (the empirical correlation between monetary growth and price inflation is a good example).

In Friedman's approach the criteria for acceptance or rejection of hypotheses are thus strictly empirical. Unlike his teacher Wesley Mitchell, however, Friedman was by no means opposed to abstract theory *per se*. In fact, one of his objectives in this essay was precisely to defend the abstract nature of neo-classical economic theory, which was often criticized due to its lack of realistic assumptions. Friedman thought these critiques were misplaced, and that scientific hypotheses should not be judged by the realism of their assumptions, since these can never be "realistic" in a descriptive sense. In fact,

> ... the relation between the significance of a theory and the "realism" of its "assumptions" is almost the opposite of that suggested by the view under criticism. Truly important and significant hypotheses will be found to have "assumptions" that are wildly inaccurate descriptive representations of reality, and, in general, the more significant the theory, the more unrealistic the assumptions (in this sense).[11] The reason is

---

[11] He was quick to add that "the converse of this proposition does not of course

simple. A hypothesis is important if it "explains" much by little, that is, if it abstracts the common and crucial elements from the mass of complex and detailed circumstances surrounding the phenomena to be explained and permits valid predictions on the basis of them alone (p. 14).

Theoretical assumptions are simplifications of reality, and in this sense they *must* be descriptively false (i.e., they take into account only the features regarded as important, since the success of the hypothesis shows that all other circumstances are irrelevant to the explanation of the phenomenon). To Friedman, the realism of the assumptions was unimportant, and "the relevant question to ask about the 'assumptions' of a theory is not whether they are descriptively 'realistic,' for they never are, but whether they are sufficiently good approximations for the purpose in hand," which can be determined only by "seeing whether the theory works, which means whether it yields sufficiently accurate predictions" (p. 15).

The "Methodology" essay was (and still remains) quite controversial, and it generated a large secondary literature.[12] Friedman, however, having

---

hold: assumptions that are unrealistic (in this sense) do not guarantee a significant theory" (p. 14n).

[12]See Boland (1979) for a good review of the early critical literature. Most economists nowadays would probably agree with Mayer that Friedman's essay is best interpreted as "an attempt to provide practicing economists with some useful ground rules, specifically with a way of healing the unfortunate split between theoretical and empirical economics that prevailed [at the time] ... Friedman aimed to provide a useful heuristic for working economists and not a sophisticated philosophical analysis .... and [his] essay is broadly consistent with the methodology that most economists now affirm, at least in principle" (Mayer, 1993, pp. 213-14). Very few working scientists ever pay much attention to what philosophers have to say about science (or about anything, for that matter), so it is not surprising that criticisms from that corner have never made much of a dent in this essay's appeal, which is not to say it is above reproach. In fact, it has been subjected to devastating criticism, and not from a philosopher but, fittingly, from an economist (and a *Chicago* economist, no less!): "The view that the worth of a theory is to be judged solely by the extent and accuracy of its predictions seems to me wrong .... Except in the most exceptional circumstances, the data required to test the predictions of a new theory ... will not be available or, if available, will not be in the form required for the tests and, ..., will need a good deal of manipulation of one sort or another before they can be made to yield the requisite predictions. And who will be willing to undertake these arduous investigations? .... [F]or the tests to be worthwhile, someone has to believe in the theory, at least to the extent of believing that it might well be true .... If all economists followed Friedman's principles in choosing theories, no economist could be found who

stated his case, preferred to let others argue about it, and never responded to any of his critics. Instead, he decided to move on, and was more concerned with applying his principles in practice.

3. Monetary Studies.

Since about 1950 his interests began to center on monetary economics, and in this field he achieved his greatest prominence. A notable collection of empirical studies edited by Friedman (*Studies in the Quantity Theory of Money*, 1956) was based on doctoral dissertations supervised in his famous Money and Banking Workshop at Chicago. A longer run project resulted from his association with the NBER, where he took charge of the monetary aspects of a much larger-scale project on business cycles. The detailed investigations related to this project resulted in three volumes co-authored with Anna J. Schwartz: *A Monetary History of the United States* (1963), *Monetary Statistics of the United States* (1970), and *Monetary Trends in the United States and the United Kingdom* (1982).

The theoretical framework underlying this empirical research, and the link to previous monetary traditions at Chicago, was Friedman's introduction to the *Studies* volume: "The Quantity Theory of Money—A Restatement" (Friedman, 1956).[13] Friedman interpreted the Quantity

---

believed in a theory until it had been tested, which would have the paradoxical result that no tests would be carried out ... [so] acceptance of Friedman's methodology would result in the paralysis of scientific activity. Work would certainly continue, but no new theories would emerge" (Coase, 1988, pp. 64, 71). Though I am myself a convinced Friedman-type positivist, I must admit that I do not know how to respond to this critique.

[13]In the "Restatement" essay Friedman stressed the Chicago roots of his approach to the quantity theory, though Patinkin (1969) later criticized him for trying to link his own theoretical contributions to an allegedly quite different "oral tradition" at Chicago. Johnson (1971) went further, imputing questionable motives and actually accusing Friedman of "scholarly chicanery" (p. 11). Friedman responded that "I shall not defend my 'Restatement' as giving the 'flavor of the oral tradition' at Chicago in the sense that the details of my formal structure have precise counterparts in the teachings of Simons and Mints. After all, I am not unwilling to accept some credit for the theoretical analysis in that article. Patinkin has made a real contribution to the history of thought by examining and presenting the detailed theoretical teachings of Simons and Mints, and I have little quarrel with his presentation. But I certainly do defend my 'Restatement' as giving the 'flavor of the oral tradition' at Chicago in what seems

Theory as, essentially, a theory of the demand for money. Though the monetary authorities might control the *nominal* money supply, what really matters for the public is the *real* money supply (the money supply expressed in terms of its purchasing power). The scientific problem consists in determining the variables affecting the demand for money, i.e., the amount of real monetary balances held by the public. According to Friedman, the demand for money is a stable function of real income and the opportunity cost of holding money. This idea and its implications were later explored empirically in Friedman (1959) and Friedman and Schwartz (1963a).

The stability of the demand for money had certain implications concerning effects of variations in the money supply that were inconsistent with the Keynesian analysis that prevailed at the time. The frontal assault on Keynesian theory appeared in an extensive empirical study (Friedman and Meiselman, 1963) which compared two basic theories: (1) a Keynesian multiplier model, relating national income to "autonomous" expenditures (investment, government spending, and net exports), and (2) a "monetarist" model (the term had not yet been invented), relating income to the money supply via the velocity of money. The results showed that in practice the money supply had far greater explanatory power than autonomous expenditures. The Friedman-Meiselman study set off the "Keynesian-Monetarist" debate that came to dominate discussions of macro-economic policy for many years.[14]

The main conclusions from this and later "monetarist" studies were that: (1) though increased public spending has an impact-effect on nominal income, it soon "fizzles out," whereas an increase in the money supply has

---

to me the much more important sense in which, as I said, the oral tradition 'nurtured the remaining essays in' *Studies in the Quantity Theory of Money*, and my own subsequent work. And, in any event, it is clearly not a tradition that, as Johnson charges, I 'invented' for some noble or nefarious purpose" (Friedman, 1972, p. 941). The Patinkin-Johnson critique provoked considerable scholarly debate involving many authors, but, as in other cases of controversies motivated by his writings, Friedman opted to observe from the sidelines. For a good review of this literature and its background see the two articles by Leeson (1998, 2000). Patinkin was a great scholar and intellectual historian, and he seems to have felt very strongly about this matter, though in retrospect it is hard to understand what the fuss was all about, and the whole episode seems rather bizarre.

[14]In this context, it is perhaps worth mentioning that, though Friedman was quite critical of "Keynesian economics," he always expressed great respect and admiration for Keynes the economist. See, for instance, Friedman (1997).

a permanent effect; (2) the adjustment of nominal income to an increased rate of monetary growth involves "long and variable lags"; (3) in the long run an increase in the rate of monetary growth affects only the inflation rate, and has no effect on real output; (4) in the short run, however, variations in the rate of monetary growth can have devastating effects, both on prices and on real output (the most notorious example being the "Great Contraction" of 1931-33, as explained in Chapter 7 of the *Monetary History* volume).[15]

4. The Economist as Public Intellectual.

Shortly after receiving his Nobel Prize, Friedman retired from the University of Chicago, and the Friedmans moved to San Francisco, where he became associated for the rest of his life with the Hoover Institution, at Stanford University. Though he remained active in economic research for some years after retirement, most of his original scientific work had been done, and his interests shifted increasingly towards popular writing and involvement in public policy issues.

He was already well-known among the broader public as a staunch critic of government intrusions in the economy, and an exponent of the virtues of an unhampered free market, views which he had expressed in *Capitalism and Freedom* (1962), and in the tri-weekly *Newsweek* columns he wrote from 1966 to 1984. His leap to celebrity, however, came with the filming of the TV documentary series "Free to Choose" and the publication of a book with the same title (Friedman and Friedman, 1980) which eventually became a world-wide bestseller.[16]

There is no point in elaborating here on his general ideas regarding capitalism and the market economy, since these are well known. Rather, I will attempt to briefly explore some of the reasons for his remarkable success in spreading his ideas to the broader public.

Part of his success as a communicator was probably due to the fact that his rhetorical style was much less ideologically-driven than that of other free-market advocates. Though he himself had a strong ideological com-

---

[15]For two brief and relatively non-technical summaries of his monetary studies, see Friedman (1968, 1970).

[16]On the impact of *Free to Choose* see the papers collected in the Dallas Fed *festschrift* (Wynne, Rosenblum and Formaini, 2004), and especially the paper by Boettke (2004).

mitment to values such as personal liberty and individual responsibility, his arguments on specific policy issues tended to stress practical matters, such as economic efficiency and how government interventions often led to consequences that were worse than the evils they sought to avoid. This approach allowed many people to agree with him on specific issues, even though they might not coincide with his entire social philosophy. Related to this is what we might call his "incremental" approach to the ideal of a free-market economy. Many policy issues are not a matter of "all or nothing" but of "more or less," and Friedman was often quite willing to settle for a compromise solution if it offered a clear possibility of moving closer to the free market ideal.

A good example is his active role in the movement which eventually ended the military draft in the United States. This was not an abstract question of "capitalism, take it or leave it," but a very specific policy issue with enormous implications for the personal liberty of millions of flesh and blood individuals. It was also an issue that, at the time and in the midst of an unpopular war, could enlist the support of many people across the whole political spectrum.[17]

---

[17]For an early statement of his views in this regard see Friedman (1967). On the role of Milton Friedman and many other prominent economists in the 1969 "President's Advisory Commission on an All-Volunteer Force" (also known as the "Gates Commission") and other initiatives that eventually resulted in the ending of the draft, see Henderson (2005). (This paper should be required reading for every American male on his 18th birthday. It is available online at: www.econjournalwatch.org). There is an interesting anecdote related to the Gates Commission hearings that is worth retelling. Among economists, Friedman had a reputation as the best stand-up debater in the profession. This was discovered the hard way by General William Westmoreland, formerly commander of U.S. forces in Vietnam:

> Like almost all military men who testified, [Westmoreland] testified against a volunteer armed force. In the course of his testimony, he made the statement that he did not want to command an army of mercenaries. I stopped him and said, "General, would you rather command an army of slaves?" He drew himself up and said, "I don't like to hear our patriotic draftees referred to as slaves." I replied, "I don't like to hear our patriotic volunteers referred to as mercenaries." But I went on to say, "If they are mercenaries, then I, sir, am a mercenary professor, and you, sir, are a mercenary general; we are served by mercenary physicians, we use a mercenary lawyer, and we get our meat from a mercenary butcher" (Friedman and Friedman, 1998, p. 380).

Whether the general had anything else to say, after he picked his head up from the

Another example is his school-voucher proposal, elaborated in Chapter 6 of *Capitalism and Freedom*, and based on an earlier paper (Friedman, 1955). Under this system the government would, ideally, no longer be involved in the actual administration of educational institutions, though it would still be involved in the financing of education, so it is not a purely free-market solution. On the other hand, it was clearly a "step in the right direction," from Friedman's point of view.[18] By separating government financing of education from government operation of schools, he argued, parents at all income levels would have greater freedom in choosing the schools their children attend. Moreover, one does not have to accept Friedman's ultimate vision of a purely private market in education in order to appreciate the efficiency and welfare-enhancing features of the "intermediate" voucher solution: more choice would involve greater competition, and hence greater efficiency in school provision.[19]

Finally, another likely factor that explains his greater success in spreading his ideas, especially among professional economists, is that Friedman (and Chicago economists in general) used essentially the same language as most mainstream economists. Indeed, as Israel Kirzner noted many years ago:

> The price theory that underlies the contributions of the "Chicago" writers is not fundamentally different from that accepted by American economists generally, including those holding the efficiency and justice of the market system in deep mistrust. It is merely that the "Chicago" economists apply their price theory more consistently and more resolutely, assigning to it a scope of relevance far wider than that granted by others .... "Chicago" price theory, like that taught in most United States economics departments, is solidly in the Anglo-American neoclassical tradition associated most importantly with Alfred Marshall (Kirzner, 1967, p. 102).

---

floor, is not reported. In any case, "that was the last we heard from [him] about mercenaries."

[18]"Murray [Rothbard] used to call me a statist because I was willing to have government money involved. But I see the voucher as a step in moving away from a government system to a private system" (Doherty, 1995, p. 36). The reference for the Rothbard critique is Rothbard (2002 [1971]).

[19]On the progress of the voucher idea in the half-century since Friedman's initial proposal, see the papers collected in Enlow and Ealy (2006). The "choice in schooling" issue was near and dear to Friedman's heart, and in 1996 he and Rose established the Milton and Rose D. Friedman Foundation, with the sole purpose of furthering the range of options for parental choice in education.

In this sense, to use a bit of economic jargon, one might say that Friedman had a "comparative advantage" in communicating with mainstream economists, as compared to other leading classical liberal economists such as Ludwig von Mises and F. A. Hayek, whose "Austrian School" background was much more alien to other members of the profession.

Of course, these are my personal impressions and conjectures, and I may be quite wrong in my interpretation of the reasons for Friedman's phenomenal success as social critic and policy advocate. Whatever the reasons for his success, however, the fact itself is indisputable.

5. A Personal Reminiscence.

A couple of years ago Alan Greenspan prepared a foreword to a collection of essays honoring Milton and Rose Friedman, and in that foreword he wrote the following:

> My first contact with Milton was in 1959, when I mailed him a copy of an article on the impact of the ratio of stock prices to replacement cost on capital investment. I am sure he had never heard of me, yet he took the time to reply with several very thoughtful suggestions. I have never forgotten that (Greenspan, 2004, p. xii).

This was not the first time I had heard or read about similar experiences, and I do not think they are isolated cases. In fact, Greenspan's experience reflects an important aspect of Friedman's personality. He was very generous with his time, even to complete strangers, and I can attest to this personally.

I too once maintained a correspondence with Milton Friedman. The first time I wrote him was to comment on one of his *Newsweek* articles. At that time, I lived in Bolivia, and was working at a sugar mill. Of course, I did not expect him to reply. Why would he? To a perfect stranger? Imagine then my surprise when I got in the mail a very polite and detailed letter in response.

I answered him, and he answered back! And that was the beginning of a correspondence that lasted several years. I even got the chance to meet him in person, soon after I began my career as a university professor. At the time I was translating some of his monetary studies. He was interested in the project, and encouraged me, and it was all by letters—no e-mail then—and since I was constantly consulting him about many minor details, at one point he suggested that maybe I should visit him, so we might sit down for a whole day with the materials and resolve all my queries. Well, I did just that. We agreed on a date, and I traveled to San Francisco and we met in his office at Stanford University.

It was a very productive meeting, although I soon realized that, though the purpose of the meeting was ostensibly to discuss his papers, he wasn't really much interested in talking about his work. Rather, he seemed much more interested in my own projects and concerns. What courses was I teaching? Had I published any papers? What other things was I working on? It so happens that I was then working on a book of my own, my first book, on Latin American inflation, and, as I recall, we actually spent more time that day talking about my book than about his own writings.

At midday he invited me to lunch at the Faculty Club (we were joined by George Stigler), and in the afternoon we talked some more, and kept on talking until it was time for me to catch my return flight. I will always remember his gracious generosity, his encouragement, and his willingness to devote part of his valuable time to a young, budding academic. It meant the world to me.

Milton Friedman was a great economist and a fine man. He had a long and productive life. May he rest in peace.

REFERENCES

Armitage, P. "Sequential Analysis," *International Encyclopedia of the Social Sciences*, vol. 14, pp. 187-92. New York: Macmillan, 1968.

Boettke, Peter J. "Milton and Rose Friedman's 'Free to Choose' and its Impact in the Global Movement Toward Free Market Policy: 1979-2003," in Mark A. Wynne *et al.* (eds.), *The Legacy of Milton and Rose Friedman's "Free to Choose": Economic Liberalism at the Turn of the 21ˢᵗ Century*, pp. 137-52. Dallas: Federal Reserve Bank of Dallas, 2004.

Boland, Lawrence A. "A Critique of Friedman's Critics," *Journal of Economic Literature*, 17 (June 1979): 503-22.

Coase, R. H. "How Should Economists Choose?" in *Ideas, Their Origins, and Their Consequences: Lectures to Commemorate the Life and Work of G. Warren Nutter*, pp. 63-79. Washington: American Enterprise Institute, 1988.

Doherty, Brian. "Best of Both Worlds: An Interview with Milton Friedman," *Reason Magazine*, 27 (June 1995): 32-38.

Enlow, Robert C. and Lenore T. Ealy, eds. *Liberty and Learning: Milton Friedman's Voucher Idea at Fifty*. Washington: Cato Institute, 2006.

Friedman, Milton. "The Use of Ranks to Avoid the Assumption of Normality Implicit in the Analysis of Variance," *Journal of the American Statistical Association*, 32 (Dec 1937): 675-701.

———. "The Methodology of Positive Economics," in *Essays in Positive Economics*, pp. 3-43. Chicago: University of Chicago Press, 1953.

———. "The Role of Government in Education," in Robert A. Solo (ed.), *Economics and the Public Interest*, pp. 123-44. New Brunswick, NJ: Rutgers University Press, 1955.

———. "The Quantity Theory of Money—A Restatement," in M. Friedman (ed.), *Studies in the Quantity Theory of Money*, pp. 3-21. Chicago: University of Chicago Press, 1956.

———. "The Demand for Money: Some Theoretical and Empirical

Results," *Journal of Political Economy*, 67 (Aug 1959): 327-51.

———. "Why Not a Volunteer Army?" *New Individualist Review*, 4 (Spring 1967): 3-9.

———. "Money: Quantity Theory," *International Encyclopedia of the Social Sciences*, vol. 10, pp. 432-47. New York: Macmillan, 1968.

———. *The Counter-Revolution in Monetary Theory*. Occasional Paper No. 33. London: Institute of Economic Affairs, 1970.

———. "Comments on the Critics," *Journal of Political Economy*, 80 (Sept-Oct 1972): 906-50.

———. "John Maynard Keynes," *Federal Reserve Bank of Richmond Economic Quarterly*, 83 (Spring 1997): 1-23.

———. "George Joseph Stigler (January 17, 1911–December 1, 1991)," *Biographical Memoirs of the National Academy of Sciences*, vol. 76, pp. 341-59. Washington: National Academy Press, 1999.

———. "Milton Friedman," in William Breit and Barry T. Hirsch (eds.), *Lives of the Laureates*, 4th ed., pp. 65-77. Cambridge, Mass.: MIT Press, 2004.

Friedman, Milton and Rose D. Friedman. *Capitalism and Freedom*. Chicago: University of Chicago Press, 1962.

———. *Free to Choose*. New York: Harcourt Brace Jovanovich, 1980.

———. *Two Lucky People: Memoirs*. Chicago: University of Chicago Press, 1998.

Friedman, Milton and David Meiselman. "The Relative Stability of Monetary Velocity and the Investment Multiplier in the United States, 1897-1958," in *Stabilization Policies*, pp. 165-268. Englewood Cliffs: Prentice-Hall/Commission on Money and Credit, 1963.

Friedman, Milton and Anna J. Schwartz. *A Monetary History of the United States, 1867-1960*. Princeton: Princeton University Press, 1963.

———. "Money and Business Cycles," *Review of Economics and Statistics*, 45 (Feb 1963a): 32-64.

———. *Monetary Statistics of the United States*. New York: Columbia

University Press, 1970.

————. *Monetary Trends in the United States and the United Kingdom, 1867-1975*. Chicago: University of Chicago Press, 1982.

Gibbons, Jean Dickinson. *Nonparametric Methods for Quantitative Analysis*. New York: Holt, Rinehart and Winston, 1976.

Greenspan, Alan. "Remarks," in Mark A. Wynne *et al.* (eds.), *The Legacy of Milton and Rose Friedman's "Free to Choose": Economic Liberalism at the Turn of the 21ˢᵗ Century*, pp. xi-xii. Dallas: Federal Reserve Bank of Dallas, 2004.

Hammond, J. Daniel and Claire H. Hammond, eds. *Making Chicago Price Theory: Friedman-Stigler Correspondence, 1945-1957*. London: Routledge, 2006.

Hartwell, R. M. *A History of the Mont Pelerin Society*. Indianapolis, IN: Liberty Fund, 1995.

Henderson, David R. "The Role of Economists in Ending the Draft," *Econ Journal Watch*, 2 (August 2005): 362-76.

Johnson, Harry G. "The Keynesian Revolution and the Monetarist Counter-Revolution," *American Economic Review*, 61 (May 1971): 1-14.

Kirzner, Israel M. "Divergent Approaches in Libertarian Economic Thought," *Intercollegiate Review*, 3 (Jan-Feb 1967): 101-08.

Leeson, Robert. "The Early Patinkin-Friedman Correspondence," *Journal of the History of Economic Thought*, 20 (Dec 1998): 433-48.

Leeson, Robert. "Patinkin, Johnson, and the Shadow of Friedman," *History of Political Economy*, 32 (Winter 2000): 733-63.

Mayer, Thomas. "Friedman's Methodology of Positive Economics: A Soft Reading," *Economic Inquiry*, 31 (April 1993): 213-23.

Patinkin, Don. "The Chicago Tradition, the Quantity Theory, and Friedman," *Journal of Money, Credit and Banking*, 1 (Feb 1969): 46-70.

Popper, Karl. *The Logic of Scientific Discovery*. London: Hutchinson, 1959. [Original German edition: *Logik der Forschung*, 1934.]

Reder, Melvin W. "Chicago Economics: Permanence and Change," *Journal of Economic Literature*, 20 (March 1982): 1-38.

Rees, Mina. "The Mathematical Sciences and World War II," *American Mathematical Monthly*, 87 (Oct 1980): 607-21.

Rothbard, Murray N. "Milton Friedman Unraveled," *Journal of Libertarian Studies*, 16 (Fall 2002): 37-54. [Originally published in *The Individualist*, 3 (Feb 1971): 3-7.]

Rowley, Charles K. "Five Market-Friendly Nobelists: Friedman, Stigler, Buchanan, Coase, and Becker," *Independent Review*, 3 (Winter 1999): 413-31.

Samuelson, Paul A. "Economics in a Golden Age: A Personal Memoir," in Gerald Holton (ed.), *The Twentieth-Century Sciences: Studies in the Biography of Ideas*, pp. 155-70. New York: W. W. Norton & Co., 1972.

————. "Complementarity: An Essay on the 40th Anniversary of the Hicks-Allen Revolution in Demand Theory," *Journal of Economic Literature*, 12 (Dec 1974): 1255-89.

Schultz, Henry. *The Theory and Measurement of Demand*. Chicago: University of Chicago Press, 1938.

Stigler, George. *Memoirs of an Unregulated Economist*. New York: Basic Books, 1988.

Tsujimura, Kotaro and Sakiko Tsuzuki. "A Reinterpretation of the Fisher-Friedman Definition of Complementarity." Keio Economic Observatory Occasional Paper No. 22. Keio University, Japan (June 1998).

Wallis, W. Allen. "The Statistical Research Group, 1942-1945," *Journal of the American Statistical Association*, 75 (June 1980): 320-30.

Wynne, Mark A., Harvey Rosenblum and Robert L. Formaini, eds. *The Legacy of Milton and Rose Friedman's "Free to Choose": Economic Liberalism at the Turn of the 21st Century*. Dallas: Federal Reserve Bank of Dallas, 2004.

7

MILTON FRIEDMAN ON INCOME INEQUALITY

Abstract

There is a certain tension in Milton Friedman's views on the issue of "freedom vs. equality," which were much more nuanced than is commonly assumed. On the one hand, he argued that economic policy should focus on freedom as a primary value, since stressing equality *per se* could lead to economic inefficiency, as well as jeopardizing freedom itself. On the other hand, he famously advocated government sponsored poverty-alleviation via the "negative income tax," a form of income redistribution which is inconsistent with his general theory of the free-market economy. His justification for this policy, however, was not on egalitarian grounds. Rather, his main motivation seems to have been compassion.

Introduction

A society that puts equality—in the sense of equality of outcome—ahead of freedom will end up with neither equality nor freedom .... On the other hand, a society that puts freedom first will, as a happy by-product, end up with both greater freedom and greater equality.[1]

It seems pretty obvious where libertarians stand on the question of "freedom vs. equality," and this quotation from Milton Friedman sums it up quite clearly: Libertarians believe that we should be concerned about

Published originally in *Journal of Markets and Morality*, 11 (Fall 2008): 239-53.

[1]Milton and Rose D. Friedman, *Free to Choose* (New York: Harcourt Brace Jovanovich, 1980), p. 148.

freedom, and nothing else. If we aim for freedom we will also get, indirectly, a good measure of equality as part of the bargain, but that is a bonus; if we aim for equality directly, however, we will lose liberty, and we will not get equality anyway.

Whether Friedman was right or not—that is, whether capitalism does in fact result in less inequality, as he claimed—is a question that presumably can be settled by research. The intriguing question, however, is why a libertarian such as Milton Friedman should be concerned with inequality at all. Note the phrasing of our initial quotation. Rhetoric apart, why would "both greater freedom and greater equality" be a "happy" by-product for Friedman, unless he valued equality for its own sake, as well as valuing liberty? Of course, we know that he probably valued the latter much more that he did the former, but still, the phrasing is subtle and suggestive, and his views on this subject might bear a closer reading.

Friedman's Case against Equality of Outcomes

Friedman's views on income inequality are most clearly stated in *Capitalism and Freedom* (1962) and in *Free to Choose* (1980), his two major popular books. In both works he starts out by arguing that we should indeed be unconcerned about income inequality in a free-market economy, and he provides three major reasons: (1) Some degree of inequality is actually desirable in any well-functioning economic system; (2) in any case, a certain degree of inequality is unavoidable under an economic system based on free-market principles; and (3) the actual degree of income inequality in observed market economies, such as the United States, is much less that is commonly assumed (especially when compared to income distributions in non-market economies).

Regarding the first two points, Friedman expresses the ethical principle behind the distribution of incomes in a market economy: "To each according to what he and the instruments he owns produces."[2] That is, and to use a bit of economic jargon, in such an economy individuals are rewarded in proportion to how much the factors of production under their control (including their own labor) contribute to total economic output. Incomes, in short, derive from property ownership and/or from work performed, and since individuals will differ in tastes and preferences, including relative preferences for leisure and for risk-taking, the principle

---

[2]Milton Friedman, *Capitalism and Freedom* (Chicago: University of Chicago Press, 1962), pp. 161-62.

of "payment in accordance with product" will necessarily result in inequalities of money incomes. Such differentials, however, are necessary in order to provide incentives for certain types of irksome or tedious labor, and for certain types of risky activities that would not be performed otherwise.[3]

Friedman goes on to note, however, that a large part of observed income inequality is not due to these "equalizing differences," as he calls them, but rather to "initial differences in endowment, both of human capacities and of property."[4] Most people do not regard inequalities due to differences in inherited personal talents and capacities as negatively as those arising from inherited wealth, though Friedman argues that the distinction is in fact untenable:

> Much of the moral fervor behind the drive for equality of outcome comes from the widespread belief that it is not fair that some children should have a great advantage over others simply because they happen to have wealthy parents. Of course it is not fair. However, unfairness can take many forms. It can take the form of the inheritance of property—bonds and stocks, houses, factories; it can also take the form of the inheritance of talent—musical ability, strength, mathematical genius. The inheritance of property can be interfered with more readily than the inheritance of talent. But from an ethical point of view, is there any difference between the two? Yet many people resent the inheritance of property but not the inheritance of talent.[5]

> Is there any greater ethical justification for the high returns to the individual who inherits from his parents a peculiar voice for which there is a great demand than for the high returns to the individual who inherits property? .... A parent who has wealth that he wishes to pass on to his child can do so in different ways. He can use a given sum of money to finance his child's training ... or to set him up in business, or to set up a trust fund yielding him a property income. In any of these cases, the child will have a higher income than he otherwise would. But in the first case, [it] will be regarded as coming from human capacities; in the second, from profits; in the third, from inherited wealth. Is there any basis for distinguishing among these categories of receipts on ethical grounds?[6]

---

[3]*Ibid.*, pp. 162-63.

[4]*Ibid.*, pp. 163-64.

[5]*Free to Choose*, p. 136.

[6]*Capitalism and Freedom*, p. 164.

As a parting shot, he notes that "it seems illogical to say that a man is entitled to what he has produced by personal capacities or to the produce of the wealth he has accumulated, but that he is not entitled to pass any wealth on to his children; to say that a man may use his income for riotous living but may not give it to his heirs."[7]

These are good points (especially the last one). As an ethical argument, however, most people would probably regard it as rather weak and unconvincing. One reviewer of *Free to Choose*, for instance, had this to say about Friedman's position regarding the distinction between inheritance of property and inheritance of talents:

> The answer to this question is that there is indeed a difference, and moreover a difference that must surely be known to the authors. It is that we do not attach any moral significance to unfairnesses determined by nature, whereas we do attach such significance to those determined by society. No one considers it *morally* wrong that one person is handsome and another ugly, but everyone holds it to be morally wrong when two people have incomes which, when compared, offend sensibilities or violate conventions. This is true whether those incomes are equal or not. We are morally outraged when a gangster makes as much as a law-abiding citizen and when a useless citizen has more than a useful one. Thus the moral issue is not that of equality of outcomes at all. It is the character of the arguments that we adduce in favor of, or against, any kind of social determination, be it access to justice, work, income, or whatever.[8]

Friedman himself seems to have been aware of these difficulties. Thus, having made his case, he immediately concedes that it does not amount to a positive *ethical* argument in favor of income inequalities under a

---

[7]*Ibid.*

[8]Robert Heilbroner, "The Road to Selfdom," *New York Review of Books*, 27 (April 17, 1980): 8. Oddly enough, some extreme egalitarians (the philosopher John Rawls, for instance) *do* agree with Friedman regarding the untenability of the distinction between inherited property and inherited talents, but they derive the exact opposite conclusion. Friedman thinks there is no difference between rewards derived from inherited wealth and rewards derived from inherited talents and capacities, and therefore concludes that they are equally legitimate. Rawls too thinks there is no difference between these two types of rewards, but the conclusion he draws is that *both* are therefore illegitimate. For a discussion and critique of Rawls's position see Charles Harris, "Capitalism and Social Justice," *Intercollegiate Review*, 20 (Spring/Summer 1984): 35-49.

capitalist-type system, since this requires appeal to some higher value, something beyond economics as such:

> The fact that these arguments against the so-called capitalist ethic are invalid does not of course demonstrate that the capitalist ethic is an acceptable one. I find it difficult to justify either accepting or rejecting it, or to justify any alternative principle. I am led to the view that it cannot in and of itself be regarded as an ethical principle; that it must be regarded as instrumental or a corollary of some other principle such as freedom.[9]

"Payment in accordance with product," as he puts it, is necessary for allocative efficiency in a market economy, but this is not in itself an ethical criterion. It can *explain* income differentials, but it cannot justify them. Freedom, on the other hand, *is* an ethical value in its own right. Acceptance of this value, however, implies acceptance of whatever income inequalities that may arise from voluntary market transactions, as well as inequalities due to inter-generational wealth transfers (since these arise, ultimately, from people's freedom to dispose of their own incomes as they see fit).

Income Inequality under Capitalism (as Compared to Alternative Systems)

How large are these resulting inequalities, and how do they compare with observed income distributions in non-capitalistic societies? This brings us to Friedman's third main line of argument, and here he treads on firmer ground, since this is a factual matter, and the facts appear to bear him out.

Given the observed diversity among human beings—in tastes and preferences, in talents and capacities, as well as in initial endowments—it should come as no surprise that the logic of income distribution under capitalism results in significant inequality of money incomes.[10] However, Friedman points out, "[t]his fact is frequently misinterpreted to mean that capitalism and free enterprise produce wider inequality than alternative systems and, as a corollary, that the extension and development of

---

[9]*Capitalism and Freedom*, pp. 164-65.

[10]"A capitalist system involving payment in accordance with product can be, and in practice is, characterized by considerable inequality of income and wealth" (*ibid.*, p. 168).

capitalism has meant increased inequality."[11]

In fact, income distributions in market economies do not compare unfavorably with those of non-market economies, even with those of socialist-type systems that are ostensibly predicated on explicitly egalitarian premises. (Not to mention the fact that *absolute* standards of living are much higher in market economies, so the incidence and extent of absolute poverty is correspondingly much lower.) Thus, Friedman argued that income inequality in the Soviet Union was actually greater than in many capitalist countries:

> Russia is a country of two nations: a small privileged upper class of bureaucrats, party officials, technicians; and a great mass of people living little better than their great-grandparents did. The upper class has access to special shops, schools and luxuries of all kind; the masses are condemned to enjoy little more than the basic necessities. We remember asking a tourist guide in Moscow the cost of a large automobile that we saw and being told, "Oh, those aren't for sale; they're only for the Politburo." Several recent books by American journalists document in great detail the contrast between the privileged life of the upper classes and the poverty of the masses.[12]

---

[11]*Ibid.*

[12]*Free to Choose*, pp. 146-47. Friedman, ever the cautious scholar and scientist, was reluctant to make a categorical statement in *Capitalism and Freedom* regarding income distribution in communist economies, due to "paucity and unreliability of evidence" at the time that book was written. His appraisal of the known facts as of 1962 was therefore somewhat guarded: "But if inequality is measured by differences in levels of living between the privileged and other classes, such inequality may well be decidedly less in capitalist than in communist countries" (p. 169). By the time *Free to Choose* was published, in 1980, much more information was available on living conditions in the Soviet Union, though the evidence he cites there is still rather anecdotal, and based largely on journalistic accounts and his own travels. A few years after *Free to Choose* was first published, Abram Bergson, a leading expert on the Soviet economy, published a well-documented survey of the available empirical evidence on income distribution in the Soviet Union: "Income Inequality Under Soviet Socialism," *Journal of Economic Literature*, 22 (Sept 1984): 1052-99. Bergson's numerical data confirmed Friedman's qualitative observations and conjectures regarding income inequality in the Soviet economy. (Today, of course, we *all* know about the abysmal living conditions in Russia under communism, so harping on that fact seems like beating the proverbial dead horse. We also know that income inequalities there increased even further during the chaotic post-

In Communist China, income inequality was greater than in *most* capitalist countries:

> China, too, is a nation with wide differences in income—between the politically powerful and the rest; between city and countryside; between some workers in the cities and other workers. A perceptive student of China writes that "the inequality between rich and poor regions in China was more acute in 1957 than in any of the larger nations of the world except perhaps Brazil."[13]

Government Measures to Alter the Distribution of Income

Having stated his general case, Friedman then proceeds to analyze several specific government interventions that are often justified on egalitarian grounds. Though these encompass a broad range of disparate government policies, the nature of his critiques usually can be reduced to

---

communist transition period. What is still not as well known, however, is the degree of economic inequality that prevailed there *during* the Soviet era.)

[13]*Free to Choose*, p. 147. Friedman also quoted the following statement from this same "perceptive student": "In China ... income distribution seems *very roughly* to have been the same since 1953" (quoted on p. 318, note 4). Friedman was citing from Nick Eberstadt, who in 1979 published two major articles on the Chinese economy in the *New York Review of Books*: "Has China Failed?" (April 5) and "China: How Much Success?" (May 3). To appreciate the full import of Eberstadt's statements, consider the following fact: from 1953 to 1980, the same period during which income distribution remained essentially unchanged in Mainland China, the Taiwanese economy achieved both a spectacular rise in the *level* of per capita income, and an equally impressive *decline* in income inequality (see, for instance, Ramon H. Myers, "The Economic Development of the Republic of China on Taiwan, 1965-81," in Laurence J. Lau, ed., *Models of Development: A Comparative Study of Economic Growth in South Korea and Taiwan* [San Francisco: International Center for Economic Growth, 1990], pp. 17-63, especially Figure 2.6 on p. 26). It is well-known, of course, that since about 1980 economic policy changed course in Communist China, and moved increasingly toward a free-market economic model. Income per capita has risen spectacularly since then, and poverty, though certainly not eliminated, has been greatly reduced. Indeed, given China's huge population, the reduction in poverty there has been so great that it alone accounts for a large share of the reduction in the *worldwide* poverty rate over the past two decades (see, for instance, Shaohua Chen and Martin Ravallion, "How Have the World's Poorest Fared since the Early 1980s?" *World Bank Research Observer*, 19 [Fall 2004]: 141-69).

two main points: (1) These policies tend to distort incentives, resulting in a less efficient allocation of resources (i.e., economic waste), and (2) they do not in fact result in major reductions of income inequality—indeed, they often have, perversely, the opposite effect.

The *progressive income tax*, for instance, has introduced many distortions in the economy, but it has not had a very large impact on the actual distribution of after-tax incomes. Friedman conjectures that this is partly due to increased inequality in the distribution of pre-tax incomes (thus partially cancelling the equalizing effect of the tax schedule), but mostly to the effect of loopholes that allow for tax avoidance. In practice, these opportunities are usually available only for large incomes (e.g., tax-free municipal bonds), and their net effect is to reduce the effective tax rates far below the nominal rates. This reduction in effective taxation is achieved, however, "at the cost of a great waste of resources, and of the introduction of widespread inequity," since the existence of loopholes "make[s] the incidence of the taxes capricious and unequal. People at the same economic level pay very different taxes depending on the accident of the source of their income and the opportunities they have to evade the tax."[14]

Public housing and *urban renewal* projects are proposed and defended as a poverty-reduction device, though Friedman argues that the net effect has been to actually *increase* inequality. Though some poor people do indeed obtain better housing, others are merely displaced to even worse conditions, since more housing is destroyed than is built:

> Far from improving the housing of the poor … public housing has done just the reverse. The number of dwelling units destroyed in the course of erecting public housing projects has been far larger than the number of new dwelling units constructed. But public housing as such has done nothing to reduce the number of persons to be housed. The effect of public housing has therefore been to raise the number of persons per dwelling unit. Some families have probably been better housed than they would otherwise have been—those who were fortunate enough to get occupancy of the publicly built units. But this has only made the problem for the rest all the worse, since the average density of all together went up.[15]

---

[14]*Capitalism and Freedom*, pp. 172-73.

[15]*Ibid.*, p. 179. In *Free to Choose*, Friedman reiterates this "displacement" effect, and adds a clincher: the main beneficiaries of public housing are the non-poor, namely, owners of property purchased for renewal projects, and people who make money building them, such as contractors, bankers, labor unions, and suppliers of

Minimum wage laws also have a perverse effect on poverty and income inequality, and this effect also involves a sort of displacement. Some lucky workers will get higher wages, but others will become unemployed:

> ... insofar as minimum wage laws have any effect at all, their effect is clearly to increase poverty. The state can legislate a minimum wage rate. It can hardly require employers to hire at that minimum all who were formerly employed at wages below the minimum. It is clearly not in the interest of employers to do so. The effect of the minimum wage is therefore to make unemployment higher than it otherwise would be .... the people who are rendered unemployed are precisely those who can least afford to give up the income they had been receiving, small as it may appear to the people voting for the minimum wage.[16]

Farm price supports are predicated on the belief that farmers, as a group, have below-average incomes. This may have been true at the time they were first established, though it would be hard to make the case nowadays in most developed countries. Even if it were still true, however, Friedman argues that "farm price supports do not accomplish the intended purpose of helping the farmers who need help," because (1) the benefits are received in proportion to the amount sold on the market, so the largest benefits go to the wealthiest farmers, and (2) the benefits that farmers actually receive are smaller than the total amounts spent: "This is clearly true of the amount spent for storage and similar costs which does not go to the farmer at all—indeed the suppliers of storage capacity and facilities may well be the major beneficiaries."[17] This policy, then, amounts to a clear case of welfare-for-the-well-off: tremendous distortions in the price system and an appalling waste of resources in order to provide benefits for people who are not particularly poor.[18]

The *welfare system*—"a rag-bag of well over 100 federal programs that have been enacted to help the poor"[19]—is rife with inefficiency, and

---

building materials (pp. 111-12).

[16]*Capitalism and Freedom*, pp. 180-81.

[17]*Ibid.*, p. 181.

[18]Note, in passing, that the non-farm public gets hit by a "double whammy": They pay the taxes that finance the policy, and for their pains they get the privilege of paying higher market prices for farm products. The poor are especially hard hit, because they spend a larger share of their incomes on food.

[19]*Free to Choose*, p. 108.

it creates and perpetuates perverse incentives. In Friedman's view, it is nothing but a "vast bureaucracy ... largely devoted to shuffling papers rather than to serving people. Once people get on relief, it is hard to get off," since they have "little incentive to earn income."[20] The amount of sheer waste involved is summarized in one eloquent statistic. Friedman calculated that as of the late 1970s spending on welfare programs in the United States (over and above Social Security) amounted to about $90 billion per year.[21] At the time, the "poverty line" was defined as $7,000 per year for a nonfarm family of four, and about 25 million people were estimated to live in families below that income level. Yearly spending on welfare programs therefore amounted to $3,600 per person below the poverty level—about $14,400 for a family of four, i.e., more than twice the poverty level itself. Thus, he concludes: "If these funds were all going to the 'poor,' there would be no poor left .... Clearly, this money is not going primarily to the poor. Some is siphoned off by administrative expenditures, supporting a massive bureaucracy at attractive pay scales. Some goes to people who by no stretch of the imagination can be regarded as indigent."[22]

This is a poignant list of indictments, and it is a wonder that anyone still takes these policies seriously. (Perhaps no one really does.) As noted above, and notwithstanding his initial statement of unconcern for inequality *per se*, Friedman's criticisms of these policies are two-pronged: (1) He criticizes them on market grounds, pointing out inefficiencies in resource allocation. (2) In addition, however, he makes the point that, though the justifications for these policies often appeal to egalitarian values, in practice they do not deliver: The desired equality is not in fact achieved, and the only real result is costly waste of resources.

Now, this second aspect of his argument might be interpreted as simply a good rhetorical tactic. Appealing to one's opponents' own values in order to defuse their policy proposals is indeed a masterly application of practical dialectics.[23] To apply this tactic effectively, moreover, one

---

[20]*Ibid.*, p. 107.

[21]*Ibid.*, p. 108. Spending on Social Security amounted to about $130 billion. Friedman had some pretty harsh things to say about Social Security as well (pp. 102-07).

[22]*Ibid.*, p. 108. I have taken the liberty of correcting a minor numerical mistake in Friedman's calculation.

[23]As Paul Samuelson once observed (in a discussion of Friedman, no less, though

need not share one's opponents' values. It is enough merely to show that they are inconsistent *on their own terms.*

Which raises the question: Is this what Friedman is doing? Merely poking holes in his opponents' logic? Or did he in fact share their concern with equality as a valid social goal, and was simply criticizing their practical implementation of a shared ideal? If he was really as unconcerned with economic inequality as he would have us think, then having made his case he could have rested it there. He would have no reason to go further, and actually propose an *effective* policy to achieve, in practice, the goals which the piecemeal interventions he criticized failed to achieve.

But this is what he proceeds to do.

The Negative Income Tax

Friedman proposed his idea of a "negative income tax" as a poverty alleviation measure, and as an alternative to all other existing government programs. It would require the government to tax family incomes above a certain minimum (B), but to provide cash subsidies (hence the expression "negative tax") to families with incomes below that minimum, as a supplement to their own earnings, with payments increasing as an inverse function of family income, up to a maximum amount of subsidy (G), corresponding to a family with zero earnings. This maximum amount of subsidy could be interpreted then as a floor below which no family's disposable income could fall. Subsidies would decrease with rising family income, falling to zero as earned income approaches B.[24]

One advantage of this scheme is that it would not require any separate administrative apparatus, since it could be managed through the existing tax system. Indeed,

[It] would fit directly into our current income tax system and could be

---

in a quite different context): "The art of jujitsu is to direct your opponent's strength against himself" ("Theory and Realism: A Reply," *American Economic Review,* 54 [Sept 1964]: 736).

[24]This is not the place for a full description of the negative income tax and its technicalities. Friedman tried to explain the idea in very simple terms (*Capitalism and Freedom,* pp. 191-94; *Free to Choose,* pp. 120-23), though his discussion is actually rather hard to follow on a first reading. The best short treatment that I have seen is by Harold W. Watts, "Negative Income Tax," in John Eatwell *et al.* (eds.), *The New Palgrave: A Dictionary of Economics* (London: Macmillan, 1987), vol. 3, pp. 622-24.

administered along with it. The present tax system covers the bulk of income recipients and the necessity of covering all would have the by-product of improving the operation of the present income tax. More important, if enacted as a substitute for the present rag bag of measures directed at the same end, the total administrative burden would surely be reduced.[25]

This alone would be an improvement. In addition, however, many economists agree that this is indeed a better way to attack poverty (which is just one aspect of income inequality, albeit the one that most people are really most concerned about). It is more effective in meeting the needs of the poor, and much more economically efficient, both in terms of resources (since it targets the poor, and them alone) and in terms of incentives (the persons receiving income subsidies have no perverse incentive to forego gainful employment, since they keep a portion of any extra income they manage to earn on their own, just like any other taxpayer[26]). Not least, it really does reduce income inequality.

It is all of these things. It is also quite incompatible with the theory of a pure free-market economy, since it is clearly a government intervention designed to alter the allocation of resources that would have resulted from voluntary exchanges between individuals acting freely in their own best interests. Like it or not, it is a policy of income redistribution—an effective one, to be sure—which involves taking from some, by force, in order to give to others.

Can such a policy be justified under Friedman's logic of individual liberty, the logic of free-market capitalism? I do not think it can, but he

---

[25]*Capitalism and Freedom*, pp. 192-93 (see also *Free to Choose*, pp. 122-23). Friedman may have underestimated some of the practical issues of implementation. For a discussion of practical aspects (and a rather negative assessment overall) see Jodie T. Allen, "Negative Income Tax," in David R. Henderson (ed.), *The Fortune Encyclopedia of Economics* (New York: Warner Books, 1993), pp. 333-37.

[26]Though the effect on work incentives for subsidy-recipients is clear, some economists think that the overall effect on total labor-supply is ambiguous, since it is possible that some workers not previously on welfare might decide to work less, given the option of an income subsidy under a negative income tax scheme. The total number of people receiving subsidies might therefore be larger than under a conventional welfare system. A large literature has accumulated on the negative income tax and its effect on work incentives. A good up-to-date review is that by Robert A. Moffitt, "The Negative Income Tax and the Evolution of U.S. Welfare Policy," *Journal of Economic Perspectives*, 17 (Summer 2003): 119-40.

does propose it, and ardently. This means, however, that he must appeal to some other value, apart from individual liberty. As a fundamental value, liberty alone will not suffice.

It could be that, by proposing a more efficient alternative to the existing welfare system, Friedman was merely making a concession to political reality. In a welfare state, redistributionist policies *will* be implemented, one way or another, so we might as well design such policies efficiently. Was it just this, however? Was it merely a case of good applied economics? Why then go out of his way to not only recommend an efficient policy, but to actually *justify* it on normative grounds?

Friedman's Justification for Government-Sponsored Poverty Alleviation

His justification for poverty alleviation, as a government policy, is by analogy with the more general argument for government intervention based on the existence of so-called "public goods" and the associated "free-rider" problem. He starts out by stating that things would (of course) be better if the problem of poverty could be resolved entirely through private charity. However, he notes:

> It can be argued that private charity is insufficient because the benefits from it accrue to people other than those who make the gifts—again, a neighborhood effect.[27] I am distressed by the sight of poverty; I am benefited by its alleviation; but I am benefited equally whether I or someone else pays for its alleviation; the benefits of other people's charity therefore partly accrue to me. To put it differently, we might all of us be willing to contribute to the relief of poverty, provided everyone else did. We might not be willing to contribute the same amount without such assurance. In small communities, public pressure can suffice to realize the proviso even with private charity. In the large impersonal communities that are increasingly coming to dominate our society, it is much more difficult for it to do so. *Suppose one accepts, as I do, this line of reasoning as justifying governmental action to alleviate poverty ....* There remain the questions, how much and how. I see no way of deciding "how much" except in terms of the amount of taxes we ... are willing to impose on ourselves for the purpose.[28]

---

[27]In *Capitalism and Freedom* Friedman often used the expression "neighborhood effect" to refer to what nowadays are usually described as "externalities."

[28]*Capitalism and Freedom*, p. 191 (italics added).

The "how" is of course the negative income tax, which is a better way to alleviate poverty than through the existing welfare apparatus (or via minimum wages, farm price supports, public housing, etc.). What is significant about this passage, however, is not the "how" but the "why." Clearly, Friedman thought that government-financed poverty alleviation was a worthy objective in its own right. His justification, however, was not on egalitarian grounds of "equality" as an end in itself. For Friedman, the libertarian, this motivation had no appeal. What did appeal to him, apparently, was compassion.[29]

Conclusion

To a hard-core libertarian, there is nothing problematic about income distribution in a market economy. The market's distribution of income is what it is, and that is all there is to it. Whether such a distribution is equal or unequal is neither here nor there. Friedman liked to pose as a hard-core libertarian, and yet he was also quite willing to allow for government intervention to reduce poverty. This creates some tension in his writings on the subject of economic inequality. Friedman was aware of this tension, and was even somewhat apologetic about it. Thus, he writes,

> The liberal will therefore distinguish sharply between equality of rights and equality of opportunity, on the one hand, and material equality or equality of outcome on the other.[30] He may welcome the fact that a free society in fact tends toward greater material equality than any other yet tried. But he will regard this as a desirable by-product of a free society, not its major justification .... He will regard private charity directed at helping the less fortunate as an example of the proper use of freedom. *And he may approve state action toward ameliorating poverty* as a more effective way in which the great bulk of the community can achieve a

---

[29]My colleague, Dr. Andrés Marroquín, has pointed out that in Friedman's case *empathy* might be a better word than mere compassion. Indeed, Friedman knew what it was like to be poor, since he had experienced poverty first-hand during his childhood and early life. Moreover, he had received help, in the form of scholarships which enabled him to complete his education. On Friedman's early years see his memoirs (co-authored with his wife Rose), *Two Lucky People: Memoirs* (Chicago: University of Chicago Press, 1998).

[30]Needless to say, Friedman here does not use the term "liberal" in its contemporary, American meaning, but in the original 19th century sense of "classical liberalism."

common objective. *He will do so with regret, however, at having to substitute compulsory for voluntary action.*[31]

Is this compatible with his avowed libertarianism? Some noted libertarians thought that it was not. For instance, Murray Rothbard—a hard-core libertarian if there ever was one—argued that "it is difficult to consider [Friedman] a free-market economist at all," and a prominent item on his bill of particulars was precisely the negative income tax idea.[32] If we assume there is only one way to be a libertarian, then Rothbard was probably right. It seems a bit extreme, however, since Friedman certainly *was* a libertarian and a free-market economist by almost anyone else's definition. He just wasn't a *hard-core* libertarian.

Perhaps he was a *compassionate* libertarian. James Buchanan has argued that such a designation is an oxymoron.[33] Milton Friedman, however, may well be the exception that proves Buchanan wrong. Indeed, he may have been the original "compassionate libertarian." At least, I like to think so.

And I like him the better for it.

---

[31]*Capitalism and Freedom*, p. 195 (italics added).

[32]Murray N. Rothbard, "Milton Friedman Unraveled," *Journal of Libertarian Studies*, 16 (Fall 2002): 52. (This article was originally published in *The Individualist*, 3 [Feb 1971]: 3-7.)

[33]James M. Buchanan, *Why I, Too, Am Not a Conservative: The Normative Vision of Classical Liberalism* (Cheltenham, U.K.: Edward Elgar, 2005), p. 8. The actual expression that Buchanan uses is "compassionate classical liberal."

Addendum[1]

Milton Friedman, by William Ruger. Major Conservative and Libertarian Thinkers, vol. 19.

New York: Continuum, 2011, xvi + 227 pp. $130.00. Hardcover.

This is a fine intellectual biography of Milton Friedman, the world-famous American economist and public intellectual who died in 2006 at the ripe old age of ninety-four. William Ruger, a political scientist at Texas State University (San Marcos), does a good job of describing Friedman's scholarly contributions in the context of the major policy debates that took place within the field of economics during the 20th century, and he also attempts to evaluate their continuing influence and relevance for today's problems and concerns. Although the tone is generally admiring, it is not hagiographic. Indeed, on several occasions the author proves quite willing to criticize or qualify his subject's arguments if he feels this is necessary, a "fair and balanced" approach that adds to the book's value for readers who might be approaching Friedman's work for the first time.

Ruger starts out by providing a detailed account of Friedman's education and professional career (Chapter 1). This is a story that has been narrated before, most notably by Friedman himself in his autobiography (*Two Lucky People,* co-authored with his wife Rose and published in 1998). Although this chapter does not provide any new biographical data beyond what is available in the published record, it is nonetheless a well-crafted and useful summary of a remarkably productive life. One interesting fact that emerges from this survey is that, although the Nobel-prize winning scholar is clearly prefigured in the brilliant graduate student and young professional, nothing about the "early" Milton Friedman would have led us to anticipate that he would also one day rise to prominence as a leading spokesman for free-market economics. In fact, if anything one might have expected contrary inclinations. Thus, Ruger mentions that as a young man Friedman was described as having "very strong New Deal leanings" (pp. 8, 15), and at several points he stresses Friedman's early "Keynesian" views (pp. 16, 21-22). Since we know that by the mid-1950s his libertarian views were well-established, the question arises as to when exactly—and how and why—this very competent technical economist

---

[1]This review was published originally in *Journal of Markets and Morality*, 14 (2) (2011): 599-601.

with no strong ideological commitments suddenly decided to embark on a second career as a crusader for the market economy.

Many scholars have mentioned the importance of his participation, at the invitation of F. A. Hayek, in the founding meeting of the Mont Pelerin Society in 1947. Ruger tends to concur and (citing Daniel Hammond) notes that this was "probably the key single event in the formation of Friedman's ideology." He also argues, however, that "Friedman must already have been well down the road to classical liberalism before leaving" for the MPS meeting (p. 34), and that we will probably never know what explains his intellectual transformation because "there was no single moment when Friedman saw the classical liberal light" (p. 35). Friedman himself could not explain it; as he once put it, there was no "Saul of Tarsis moment" (p. 66). So this is a puzzle that will continue to intrigue scholars for the foreseeable future (if not forever).

Chapter 2 is devoted to reviewing Friedman's major achievements in technical economics, as well as his most important contributions to public policy debates. It also includes a fairly detailed, critical discussion of "Friedman's Political Theory" in which Ruger notes, approvingly, that "Friedman was always pragmatic in his approach to politics. In particular, he was amenable—much to the chagrin of some of his fellow libertarians—to compromises and half steps that would produce a freer society even if only incrementally .... This willingness to compromise was likely part of the reason for his unparalleled success (for a radical and a libertarian) in being taken seriously by political actors" (pp. 96-97). On the other hand, Ruger argues that Friedman's political thought was not very sophisticated, and even somewhat inconsistent:

> Friedman's political theory was not a tight philosophical system in which he resolved or even seemed to seriously grapple with the possible tensions among the values he cherished. In fact, he had little interest in wrangling with any of the fundamental philosophical issues within liberal thought, including the defense of individual freedom or material welfare as the highest ends .... One likely reason is that [he] was simply more interested in doing economics and pushing for a freer society through his engagement in public policy debates than he was in exploring the philosophical nuances of liberal thought .... [However,] it is perhaps unfair to criticize Friedman too much in this regard since he was an economist, not a political or moral philosopher, and never pretended to be otherwise. Instead, when it came to politics, he was an applied theorist and popularizer of a certain type of political thought that had been explored in more detail by others (pp. 98-99).

At one point Ruger almost seems to raise his hands in frustration: "Thus,

Friedman's position almost approached the notion that freedom is the ultimate value—except when it's not! …. Indeed, it might be impossible to impose a system on Friedman's thought other than to say he was a classical liberal" (p. 101).

Given Friedman's importance as a monetary economist, it should come as no surprise that monetary issues figure prominently in this lengthy chapter. Other subjects that are discussed in some detail include his views on the issue of school vouchers, social welfare policy and his "negative income tax" proposal, military conscription and his role in the movement to end the draft, and the thorny issue of drug policy. One other section in this chapter that might be of great interest to readers of this *Journal* is a discussion of his famous attack on the notion of the "social responsibility of business."

In the last two chapters, Ruger assesses the reception and influence of Friedman's ideas, and their contemporary relevance. He points to evidence showing that Friedman, years after his death—and *many* years after his retirement from active research—continues to influence the ideas of economists and policymakers. "But," posits Ruger, "will he be long remembered? Does Friedman have much staying power compared to other big thinkers of the twentieth century?" Very prudently, he prefers to leave this question open. Echoing Zhou Enlai on the French Revolution, he simply states that "it is much too early to tell" (p. 191).

Overall, this book is an excellent summary of a large corpus of sometimes quite technical material, and, to the author's credit, he somehow manages to do it in plain English and without using a single equation, graph or chart. The result is a highly readable account that really *can* be understood by the proverbial "educated layman." (Might this have anything to do with the fact that Ruger is a political scientist? A typical modern economist would not have resisted the temptation to spice things up with fancy footwork and technical jargon.)

The only thing that I dislike about this book is its price. It is a handsome little volume, but I am not at all convinced that it is worth $130.00, and I doubt that very many copies will be sold at that price. The other volumes in this series are similarly priced, and one has to wonder what the publishers were thinking by deciding to price themselves out of the market. (Milton Friedman, a great believer in downward-sloping demand curves, might have wondered too. Or perhaps he might have uncovered some hidden economic rationality in such a counter-intuitive decision.) Anyway, the list price for this book practically guarantees a very small market for it, which in turn means that very few people will read it. And that is a real shame.

APPENDIX — SHORTER COMMENTS AND REVIEWS

A. Review of *Just Get Out of the Way: How*   139
    Government Can Help Business in Poor Countries,
    by Robert E. Anderson

B. Review of *The Collected Works of Arthur Seldon*,   143
    vol. 1: *The Virtues of Capitalism*

C. Foreword to *Ensayos de Historia Económica*,   147
    by Gustavo A. Prado Robles

D. In Memoriam: Joseph E. Keckeissen, 1925-2011   149

E. The Achievement of Arnold Harberger   153

Just Get Out of the Way: How Government Can Help Business in Poor Countries, by Robert E. Anderson.[1]

Washington, D.C.: Cato Institute, 2004, vii + 274 pp. $24.95.

This is a very good book, though I wish it had a better title. The danger is that it might be dismissed as just another ideologically-driven "do away with the state" toolkit—the kind of books that are only convincing to people who are already of like mind, and are rarely read by the people who really need to. And that would be a shame, because this book is not about ideology at all. Instead, it is about something that is all too often missing from discussions on development policy: sound economic and business principles, consistently applied, buttressed by simple common sense and a healthy dose of pragmatism. (Are all these expressions synonymous? If not, then they should be.)

Robert Anderson, a development consultant and former World Bank economist, is a convinced free-market advocate. He takes it for granted that the only way to promote long-term economic growth in poor countries is to transfer most economic activities from the public to the private sector. However, this transfer in itself is not enough because a good "business environment" is also needed in order to encourage the private sector to function efficiently. Indeed, if the market economy works better than any other alternative, it does so not because private businesspeople are somehow better people: "Private businesspeople are not inherently more honest or more capable than government officials and politicians" (p. 6). In fact, they are just as self-serving as the rest of us ordinary humans. What makes the market economy tick is competition; without this crucial element, there is no guarantee that the resources the private sector employs will in fact be used efficiently. Echoing an insight that dates at least from the time of Adam Smith, Anderson notes that businesspeople everywhere (and not just in the Third World) are quite creative in enlisting the government's help in order to stifle competition. The trick, therefore, is not to let them get away with it. And "there's the rub," because the low levels of competence in Third World officialdom, coupled with high levels of corruption, increase the likelihood that private special-interest groups will end up manipulating government power for their own purposes. This problem should be constantly borne in mind, says Anderson, especially

---

[1]This review was published originally in *Independent Review*, 9 (3) (2005): 454-56.

when implementing policies designed to "strengthen the private sector" because the designers of these policies apparently do not seem to realize that they will be implemented in countries with weak institutional and legal structures. Most of the book is devoted to showing how policies that conceivably might work in developed countries (many of them are questionable even there) are often disastrous when transplanted to the totally different institutional contexts that prevail in poor countries.

Privatization of state-owned enterprises is a case in point. Everyone now thinks this is a good thing (Anderson does, too), and a minor industry of "experts" has arisen to peddle "advice" on privatization programs. Too often, however, these programs stress dozens of ancillary objectives that privatization is supposed to accomplish, even to the point of negating what should be the main purpose: transferring control of assets to whoever can use them most effectively and selling them for the highest price that can be obtained because these assets belong to all citizens. Instead of adopting this commonsense approach, however, governments often place mis-guided and self-defeating restrictions, such as selling only part of the company (often retaining a non-controlling share), placing limitations on foreign bidders, or conditioning the winning bid not only on the offered price but on the "quality" of the bidders' "business plans" or on the "future investments" they promise to make in the newly privatized company. Anderson argues that any departure from what he calls "best practice" privatization—that is, sell 100 percent of the company in an auction open to any and all investors, domestic or foreign, for the highest cash price—will likely result in a lower sales price for the government's assets or in opportunities for corruption and "cronyism." Bottom line: just sell it!

Throughout the book, the author emphasizes issues of corporate governance, and although the book deals for the most part with problems in developing countries, it can serve just as easily as an excellent casebook for courses on applied corporate finance. In fact, the last time I read such a concentrated dosage of good business sense was in a collection of Berkshire Hathaway shareholder reports ("Lord Bauer, meet Warren Buffett"). Anderson's discussion of bankruptcy is especially effective, and here his approach is to stick to one simple point: "a bankrupt company should continue to operate ... if its *going-concern value* exceeds its *liquidation value*. If not, the company should be liquidated, cease operations, and sell its assets to others who can make better use of them" (p. 175, italics in original). In other words, the ultimate objective should be to maximize economic efficiency (much the same objective, of course, that is ostensibly pursued in privatizing state-run enterprises). In practice, this approach amounts to steering clear of two pitfalls: on the one hand, needlessly liquidating still-viable companies, and, on the other, allowing unviable companies to continue to operate and waste resources that other firms can put to better use. What legal arrangements are best suited to minimize both of these risks? Anderson perceives a growing tendency for "many experts and international development institutions [to] support the option of a government or court-managed restructuring [of companies] in poor countries simply because it is what the rich countries do" (p. 178). He doubts that this avenue necessarily leads to the most efficient outcome even in those countries, and in developing countries it often gets resources more or less permanently "trapped in zombie companies with no economic future that are kept alive by the government" (p. 174).

Overall, one of the book's most appealing aspects is the author's willingness to call a spade a spade. Textbook theory stresses the banking system's all-important role in channeling savings into new investment. In practice, however, banks in developing countries are often little more than Ponzi games and pyramid schemes; instead of contributing to capital formation, they often squander a large proportion of savings. The main culprits, in Anderson's view, are the existence of explicit or implicit government deposit insurance and the well-known moral-hazard problems that inevitably follow. Elaborate banking regulations designed to protect the depositing public are of little avail, even in rich countries with more or less competent bureaucracies. Attempting to transplant these bank-supervision techniques to poor countries is an exercise in futility: "If [rich] countries cannot successfully implement such a system, is it plausible that poor countries can do so given their weaker governmental institutions and political systems?" (p. 141). For the latter countries, it seems, the best we can realistically hope for is the private monitoring of banks, and the best way to do that is to "eliminate deposit insurance entirely" (p. 160).

Just Get Out of the Way makes easy reading, and for a serious book on a serious subject it is often very entertaining. Anderson makes good use of the available empirical evidence, and the first three chapters contain a number of interesting tables and charts, some of which are quite eye-popping (don't miss Figure 3-4, on p. 66, a cross-country comparison of CEO compensation). The book is also peppered with interesting tidbits gleaned from the technical literature. (My personal favorite is a finance-type "event" study, published in the *Journal of Accounting and Economics*, which examined what happened to the share price of U.S. companies when their senior executives died unexpectedly, say, because of plane crashes or heart attacks. Surprisingly, share prices often increased after the deaths, which suggests a new twist on the hoary old lawyer joke: What do you call a hundred CEOs dead at the bottom of the sea? "A market rally.")

Anderson has written a thoughtful and informative analysis of the problems that developing countries currently face in their transitions to market-based economies. He has mapped some of the pitfalls to be avoided, and if his book gets the wide readership it deserves, then (one hopes) we may learn a little from our mistakes.

The Collected Works of Arthur Seldon, vol. 1: *The Virtues of Capitalism*, edited and with an introduction by Colin Robinson.[1]

Indianapolis, IN: Liberty Fund, 2005, xxx + 478 pp. $24.00.

This book is the first of a seven-volume Liberty Fund collection, designed to honor the life's work of Arthur Seldon, one of the great classical-liberal thinkers of our time. Through his own work, and through his many years of able editorial guidance at the Institute of Economic Affairs (London), Seldon was instrumental in promoting the values of a free society, mainly by espousal of sound economic analysis in a wide variety of different policy contexts. He is also well-known as the co-author (with F. G. Pennance) of the famous *Everyman's Dictionary of Economics*, which I consider the best one-volume dictionary of the subject ever made. (I still have my trusty, dog-eared "Seldon and Pennance" from student days, and I am happy to see that the projected *Collected Works* will include this classic as Volume 3.)

The main component of this first volume is a book entitled *Capitalism*, originally published in 1990 and therefore somewhat dated, though it is still worthwhile, both as a statement of his general economic philosophy, and as a primer on the shortcomings of socialism.

It is partly autobiographical, and many of the personal tidbits are quite fascinating (I wish there were more of them). At times, the material is organized more or less as a running commentary on the many IEA studies and publications that he edited during his long career. That too is interesting and helpful, though perhaps a formal survey with that sole purpose in mind would have been more useful. In addition, the author has attempted to combine these two different objectives with yet a third one—the main purpose of the book—which is to provide an overall *apologia* for what he variously describes as "the price system," "the market economy," or, more often, simply "capitalism."

Seldon's case for capitalism is richly detailed, and a short summary would barely do it justice, though if pressed I might say that "in a nutshell" what he argues is that capitalism has been given a "bad rap," mostly because it has been compared to a theoretical illusion. For too long, discussions of "capitalism versus socialism" had been carried out on an unfair playing field: all-too-visible shortcomings of *actual* capitalism were

---

[1]This review was published originally in *Journal of Markets and Morality*, 8 (2) (2005): 547-49.

contrasted with the purely theoretical virtues of *ideal* socialism. This fruitless polemic was initially abetted by the lack of reliable information regarding actual conditions in real, existing socialist economies, and later fortified by leftist intellectuals' reluctance to face the awful facts as they gradually (and inevitably) became public knowledge. Few will now deny that socialism in practice has been a sorry failure everywhere.

Seldon goes further, however, and argues that the really interesting and important comparisons are not theory versus theory, nor practice versus practice, but socialism in practice versus capitalism *in theory*. That is, we should not compare socialism (theoretical or practical) with capitalism *as it is*, but with capitalism *as it could be*: "The critics of capitalism have persisted in the device of contrasting imperfect capitalism as it is, or has been, with a vision of socialism as it has not so far been, and could not be in the foreseeable future" (p. 283). Seldon proposes instead to "match the socialist tactic of contrasting imperfect capitalism as it has been with 'perfect' socialism as they said it would be; *the opposite contrast emphasized here is of socialism as it has been with capitalism as it could be*" (p. 104, emphasis added).

(This argument should resonate today even more than when the book was first published, 15 years ago, since developments in post-Soviet Russia have created something that most market-oriented economists, only a few years ago, would have regarded as theoretically impossible: a seemingly capitalist economy that actually works *worse* than socialist planning along many significant dimensions.)

Any attempt at further summary for a short review runs the risk of over-simplification, and this would be a disservice to Seldon, who presents his arguments and marshals his facts with great skill, flair and vigor. I will only point out that Chapter 12 ("The Values of Capitalism") should be of special interest to readers of this *Journal*, and that the book includes a 30-page annotated bibliography that should prove quite useful to students interested in further exploration of these topics.

I must also note, however, that there are two aspects of the book which detract from its overall quality. For one thing, sometimes Seldon weakens his case by overstating it. One may question, for instance, whether endless harping on the evils and failures of socialism actually adds up to a positive case *for* capitalism, and whether it really addresses legitimate concerns people often have over some very specific issues. Take, for instance, the important question of the environment. It doesn't really help a lot if all we can do is point out that it is even worse under socialism (pp. 378-79). Many socialists have jumped onto the environmental bandwagon, to be sure, but not everyone who is concerned about global warming is a victim of anti-capitalist bias, nor is every environmentalist a rabid socialist.

Secondly, there is the matter of *tone*. Seldon often exhibits an air of irritable impatience with his opponents, and if I may say so, sometimes reveals a bit of a mean streak. It is not very nice, for instance, to call people "dunces" or "simpletons" (pp. 203-04) just because they disagree with you—and, what's worse, as a rhetorical strategy it is simply counter-productive. He also sometimes gets carried away by his own rhetoric. It is all very well to argue that we should be grateful for rising standards of living under capitalism, and indeed we should, but to wax poetic about the "glories" of capitalism (p. 265) might strike many people as "laying it on a bit thick." It might have been better if Seldon had simply stuck to the style of presentation that has served IEA so well over the years: dispassionate analysis based on hard evidence and cogent logic, with a minimum of ideological overtones.

But Seldon's unforgiving tone should itself be forgiven. His generation faced and overcame a hard challenge that took their civilization to the brink, only to witness later how Britain slowly became "the sick man of Europe." But he was also part of what changed all that. Seldon is one of the foremost applied economists of the 20th century. It is fitting that he be honored.

Foreword to *Ensayos de historia económica*, by Gustavo A. Prado Robles. Ensayos del Instituto de Investigaciones Económicas y Sociales "José Ortíz Mercado", vol. 3.

Santa Cruz, Bolivia: Universidad Autónoma Gabriel René Moreno, 2008.

The School of Economics at Universidad Autónoma "Gabriel René Moreno" has wisely decided to reprint these essays by Gustavo A. Prado Robles, one of his generation's most noteworthy Bolivian historians. For those of us who have followed, admiringly, his intellectual output, each one of his successive publications has been reviewed with pleasure, since they all combine the scholarship of a first rate academic with the informed judgment of an expert in the subject matter, both being the end result of a lifetime of study and reflection. The chance to have them now collected in one volume further enhances their value.

The first four of these essays deal with Bolivian economic history, and the first three specifically with the 19th century, in which Gustavo has specialized. They are important studies that illuminate a period over which debates are still ongoing. In these studies the author shares with us his deep knowledge of the source materials and of the successive interpretations they have been subjected to, and he shows us how those interpretations have evolved, both as a result of new documentary material and through the development of new "interpretive matrices" motivated by theoretical changes in economics itself. It is interesting, in effect, to observe how the very manner in which a given historical phenomenon is observed is conditioned by the observer's theoretical preconceptions, and that is why each generation must reinterpret the same facts in the light of changing knowledge. It is particularly fascinating to contrast the opinions of contemporary actors—the people who observe a given phenomenon "in real time," as it were—with the opinions of those who interpret the same phenomenon from a more distant temporal perspective. The latter observers not only have more complete information, but they also have access to theoretical tools, a set of *instruments* of interpretation, that the former did not have. Thus, understanding why the contemporary actors thought the way they did becomes an intellectual problem in its own right, a problem that not only requires an effort to understand the historical situation in its own context, but also detailed knowledge of the evolution of economic thought. Few people have the skills required for this type of investigation, and Gustavo Prado is one of them. This is especially noticeable in his commentary on *El Bosquejo del Aldeano*, a remarkable monograph written by an anonymous "doctor de Charcas" in the early years of the Bolivian republic, recently discovered and edited by Dr. Ana María Lema.

The fourth essay deals with a more recent episode of Bolivia's economic history, and was co-authored with Herbert S. Klein, who was Gustavo's teacher at Columbia University and is himself regarded as one of the world's leading English-language Bolivianists.[1] The subject of this essay—published originally in a Banco Central de Bolivia com-memorative volume[2]—is the inflation of 1952-56 and its economic and political background. Every student of Bolivian economic policy should read this essay and reflect on this episode, whose parallels with the more recent great inflation of the 1980s are quite evident and very instructive.

The last three essays are commentaries on the work of other writers, and here too Gustavo displays great scholarship and a wonderful ability to synthesize a great mass of material. His survey of the debates regarding the Industrial Revolution is a *tour de force*, practically required reading for anyone needing a quick update on the current status of this inexhaustible subject, and the essay on Douglass North is a valuable introduction to the thought of this important economist and historian. Of the three essays in this second part, however, the most remarkable, in my view, is the study of *One Hundred Years of Solitude*, where our author applies his knowledge of economic history in the service of literary criticism. Indeed, although the saga of Macondo—the story that practically defined the new genre of "magical realism"—is of course fictional, Gustavo points out nonetheless that "the foundations of its plot are predominantly historical," and he puts the tools of his trade to good use in clarifying certain elements of this justly admired novel.

I therefore recommend reading these essays, and I commend those responsible for re-issuing them in this fine collection. They have made an important contribution to Bolivian historiography, and to that of Latin America in general.

---

[1]Herbert S. Klein, *Bolivia: The Evolution of a Multi-Ethnic Society* (Oxford University Press, 1982).

[2]Gustavo A. Prado Robles and Herbert S. Klein, "La Revolución Nacional y su Impacto en el BCB: Inflación y Estabilización Monetaria Bajo el Régimen Revolucionario," in *Historia Monetaria Contemporánea de Bolivia* (La Paz: Banco Central de Bolivia, 2005), pp. 125-81.

In Memoriam:
Joseph E. Keckeissen (1925-2011)[1]

Joe Keckeissen, who died this year in Quetzaltenango, was one of the first faculty members at Universidad Francisco Marroquín, and he was a well-known member of this academic community, both at our central campus and at the extension campus in Quetzaltenango. He was an unforgettable character, and was much loved by the many generations of students he taught during almost four decades of teaching in Guatemala, his second homeland.

For Spanish-speakers, his surname was very hard to pronounce, so oftentimes his friends and acquaintances called him by a shortened version of his name, "Joe Keck." He sometimes used this version himself, and on occasions he would even sign his name this way—a generous effort to make life a little easier for his fellowman.

As an economist Joe had a close affinity to what is known as the Austrian School, and his teaching reflected the principles and theories he learned from his own teachers, among them the eminent economist Ludwig von Mises, and the equally eminent Israel Kirzner. Since UFM from the outset was identified with the economics of Mises, many of us thought at first that that was the reason why Joe came to Central America—that is, we assumed that he came to teach Austrian economics at UFM. The real story, as often happens, was a little more complicated, and to understand it we need to know some aspects of his personal biography. I will try in these few pages to delineate the essential features of this exemplary life.

Joseph Edward Keckeissen was born in Brooklyn, New York, on January 14, 1925, the son of George Wilfred Keckeissen and Rita Grace McNally. On his father's side his ancestry was German, and his mother's family was Irish. I remember that Joe was very proud of his Irish ancestry, and most certainly his firm commitment to Catholicism had its roots in his mother's family.

He was an only child, and unfortunately his parents' marriage was not a lasting one, as they were divorced when he was a small child. This was the time of the Great Depression, and since his mother needed to work, he was sent to a boarding school run by the Salesian fathers in Goshen, about

---

[1]Published originally in *Laissez-Faire*, No. 35 (2011): 83-85.

70 miles from New York City. Later, he entered a Salesian seminary, Don Bosco College, in Newton, New Jersey, where he lived for many years, finishing high school and commencing his first years of college study.

He completed his undergraduate studies in Salesian institutions, and he probably would have continued his religious studies until his final ordination as a Salesian priest, but then chance intervened. He was drafted for military service during the Korean War, in 1950, and since he was a college graduate he was sent to Officer Candidate School, and later he received specialized training, first in the artillery and later in parachute school. Indeed, Joe served in one of the most specialized branches of the armed forces: airborne artillery. This never ceased to amaze people when they first learned about this, because Joe, in his physical aspect, was the *least* military-looking person one could possibly imagine. Nonetheless, as in everything else he did in his life, he discharged his duties quite well. In fact, the Army became a second career for this humble little Salesian, and he maintained his status as a reserve officer until he retired in 1985 with the rank of lieutenant colonel.

He served with distinction in Korea, in the final stages of the conflict, and when his active service ended he used his GI Bill to study business administration at Columbia University, where he obtained an MBA in 1955. At Columbia one of his most notable teachers was Joel Dean, author of a famous textbook on managerial economics.[2] The Business School at Columbia was then—and still is—a very high-ranking institution, and he obtained there a very good technical training. But his turn towards theoretical economics came later, when he took doctoral courses at New York University and had the opportunity to attend Ludwig von Mises's famous seminar. His doctoral dissertation, which he wrote under the supervision of Israel Kirzner, is a comparative survey of the historical evolution of the concept of "economic law".[3] It is a very detailed and scholarly investigation, and I think it should be translated and published, since there is no comparable work in the Spanish language and I am sure that future generations of economists would benefit from its insights.[4]

---

[2] Joel Dean, *Managerial Economics* (New York: Prentice-Hall, 1951).

[3] Joseph E. Keckeissen, "The Meanings of Economic Law" (doctoral dissertation, New York University, 1976).

[4] [Author's note: A few years after Joe's death, I did in fact translate his dissertation, which was published in 2014 under the UFM imprint with the title *¿Qué significan las leyes económicas?*]

By the time he defended his doctoral dissertation, in 1976, he had been residing for many years in Central America. He first went to El Salvador, invited by Father Ambrosio Rossi, who had been his teacher in the Salesian seminary, and with whom he had reestablished contact after many years. Father Rossi was by then working in El Salvador, and he invited Joe to return to the Salesian community. He accepted the invitation, and in December of 1962 he arrived in San Salvador and placed himself under the orders of the Provincial of the Salesians for Central America. Some years later he met Father Angel Roncero, also a Salesian and one of the founders of Universidad Francisco Marroquín. Upon learning that Joe had studied with Mises, Father Roncero immediately realized that Joe's "comparative advantage" would be much greater teaching economics at UFM than if he stayed on in El Salvador as a high school teacher.

And that is how Joe arrived at UFM, and this was almost four decades ago. From then on he managed to balance three separate careers, all at the same time—as a soldier, as an academic economist, and as member of a religious order—earning esteem and respect from everyone who met him and had the privilege of interacting with him in the different aspects of his life. In 1989 UFM awarded him the degree of Doctor of Social Science, *honoris causa*, an honor that he always cherished. The Salesians also appreciated him, and all through his life he was deeply devoted to this religious order. In this regard, I wish to cite here from a newspaper article written by José Molina Calderón (and from which I have borrowed some of the biographical data for this note). At one point, Señor Molina tells us that Joe confessed to him one day:

> "I always felt in my heart the desire to be a Salesian; I tried to live in the spirit of the order and to collaborate with it in any way I could. That is why, in 1986, after a spiritual retreat, I decided to ask to return to the Congregation. My old novice master encouraged me; other Salesians did too. And now, on this 8th of September, 1990, I joyfully take my religious vows, once again after so many years away from home."[5]

During the last years of his life, Joe split his time between Quetzaltenango and Guatemala City, teaching university classes in both cities. In October of 2010 he suffered a stroke that left him incapacitated, and after a long illness he finally rested in the early morning of April 3, 2011.

---

[5]José Molina Calderón, "Un economista en Quetzaltenango," *Prensa Libre* (Dec 22, 2010), p. 25.

Joe Keck was a devout Catholic, a brave soldier and a great economist. How he managed to combine these diverse aspects of his life is a mystery for those of us who knew him and admired him. In addition to all of this, he was a passionate defender of the ideals of a free society.

Farewell, dear Joe. We will never forget you.

The Achievement of Arnold Harberger

I should start out by saying what a great honor it is to comment on Professor Harberger's paper. I am very grateful for the opportunity, but I should confess that when I first received the invitation I was also overcome by a sense of inadequacy. I was never a student of Harberger, nor did I ever work closely with him on any major project. (I did participate in a minor capacity on a project for policy reform in Guatemala that he led in the early 1990s, but I was just one member of a very large team, and I did not have much direct interaction with him.)

So I cannot say that I know him well. On the other hand, for a long time I have admired his style as an applied economist, and I have long been aware of his writings in several different fields, writings that I have studied with care and often cited in my own work.[1] And even though I have not myself worked in most of the areas to which he has devoted most of his career—public finance, for instance, has never been a major field of mine, nor have I done much work in project evaluation[2]—I can say that "Alito", as he is known throughout Latin America, has been a major role model for me, an experience that I know I share with many other Latin American economists of my generation.

Unfortunately, I received the draft of his presentation only recently, so I did not have time enough to prepare a detailed comment on the paper he just delivered. But over the past couple of months I have been reading and re-reading quite a bit of his published work, and what I would like to do today is comment briefly in a general way on why I think Alito has been so influential among economists and policy professionals in this part of the world—an influence, I should add, that throughout his long career has had an enormously positive effect in moving the direction of economic policy towards a greater reliance on the free-market principles that the Mont Pèlerin Society has always stood for. I will also offer some personal

---

Slightly revised version of a paper prepared for presentation at the 2015 Regional Meeting of the Mont Pèlerin Society (Lima, Peru, March 23, 2015).

[1]Two papers that I have cited many times are Harberger (1963) and Harberger (1981). I have also often cited several of the papers collected in Harberger (1984).

[2]On Harberger's contributions to these fields see Hines (2001) and Harberger (1987, 1994, 2003).

observations that come from the memories of a "lifetime Harberger observer", that I think will illustrate some of the points I will try to make.

To place his contribution in context, one has to picture first what the dominant paradigm in development economics looked like when he first came to Latin America in the mid-1950s.[3] In retrospect, when one reviews the development literature of that time, one thing that seems very striking is that the "experts" all seemed much more self-confident than they are today, and they would often formulate grandiose plans that called for major structural transformations, with a corresponding role for extensive government involvement in the economy.

Indeed, one common feature of the development models of the time is that they all involved extensive state action, not only in planning but often in the direct allocation of resources. The state was viewed as the major agent of change, and governments were expected to promote capital formation, provide employment for so-called "surplus" labor, and promote industrialization through "import-substitution"—often through direct investment of public funds.

Against these grandiose and extremely sanguine visions of what could be achieved by government action, Alito brought instead a much more humble and modest vision of what governments could achieve. He also observed that these countries were all rife with inefficiencies and economic distortions, most of them arising from misguided or poorly designed government policies.

Industrialization based on import-substitution, for instance, instead of leading to economic development through increased productivity, more often than not merely protected inefficient domestic producers by raising artificial barriers to foreign competition. Many of these countries also suffered from high inflation due to chronic government deficits financed by money creation, and this invariably led to major price distortions, as governments attempted to control the rise of certain sensitive prices. Major distortions were especially prevalent in interest rates and in currency exchange rates. All of these distortions led to reduced productivity and reduced living standards due to inefficiencies and misallocation of resources.

So instead of trying to jump-start development by implementing these overly ambitious development plans, why not start out by reducing the waste of resources? Alito not only understood the causes and consequences of these distortions, but he was also very effective in

---

[3]A good review of how the field of development economics has evolved over the second half of the 20th century is provided by Meier (2001).

explaining, often in very vivid terms, the nature of these problems and the best ways to solve them. As an illustration, I would like to share a personal anecdote, if I may. When I was still an undergraduate student, I once attended a lecture that Alito gave at Universidad Francisco Marroquín, in Guatemala. Alito was a personal friend of Manuel Ayau, the founder of our university, and he has visited our campus many times over the years. This particular visit was in the mid-1970s, and it might have been his first visit to Guatemala.

Anyway, he was telling us about the inflation in Chile during the Allende years, and how it led to pervasive price controls, the ensuing shortages, and the consequent need to subsidize certain basic commodities, such as bread, and how this led to even more distortions, because at the artificially low, subsidized prices, buyers had no incentive to allocate resources to their highest valued uses. And to illustrate this he told us something that has stuck with me to this day, 40 years later: bread was so cheap, in real terms, that for pig farmers it was cheaper to feed their hogs with bread than with corn. And this image was so shocking to me that, as I say, it has stuck with me to this day, and I can still feel the sense of outrage that I felt, that in a country that was going through a major economic crisis, scarce foreign exchange was being wasted in order to import wheat, so that pig farmers could feed their hogs with freshly baked bread.

I should add that this particular lecture probably pushed me into studying economics as a profession. I was uncertain as to what major to choose, but after that lecture I was "hooked" forever, and I am pretty sure that many other young students like me must have had the same experience. (And perhaps even with the same example, as he must have used it many times.)

In any case, Alito's lecture had a galvanizing effect on me, and his lecturing must have had a similar effect on scores, perhaps hundreds, of other students of my generation. His lectures not only imparted knowledge and information but also a sense of mission, a sense that these things should not be allowed to happen, that something should be done about it. And this sense of mission must have been especially pronounced among his first group of students during the years he spent in Chile, and even more so in the case of the group that went on to study with him at the University of Chicago—the core of the famous "Chicago Boys". Indeed, when one reads the personal memoirs of some of the "Chicago Boys"—in preparing this presentation I read, for instance, the memoirs published by Ernesto Fontaine, who died last year, I am sad to say—one thing that you get when you read these memoirs is a strong sense that, to many of Alito's students, the study of economics became not just a matter of learning how to use certain tools. It also became a commitment to using those tools to rid the world of many unnecessary evils and imperfections, a commitment to help make the world a better place. And I believe Alito was very effective in conveying this sense of mission, because he himself was committed to these ideals. This partly explains his success. To succeed in anything you have to believe in what you're doing.

I say *partly*, however, because in itself this strong sense of mission would not have been enough. Many other libertarians—quite a few of them are members of this society—are just as committed, but unfortunately they have not been anywhere nearly as successful in spreading their ideas. At least not in a policy-relevant sense. I am thinking specifically of economists who follow the Austrian School, the followers of Mises and Hayek. No one is as committed to free-market economics as these thinkers, and certainly they have made great contributions to our theoretical understanding of the market economy and how it works. And yet I am sure that everyone here would agree that, in terms of practical impact on actual policy reform, the influence of their teaching has been virtually nil.

Alito himself sets great store by what he calls "relevance" in economics. He views economic theory as a tool with real policy implications, and in his work he has always stressed the importance of basing policy analysis on observations of the real world.[4] I'm sure he is right about this, and in any kind of communication the *content* of what you have to say is certainly important. But the *way* you say it is important as well. I personally believe that one factor that explains Alito's greater success in spreading his ideas, especially among professional economists, is that he (and Chicago economists in general) has always used essentially the same language as most mainstream economists, that is, the language of neo-classical economics.

And to bolster this claim I want to cite from a very old paper by Israel Kirzner—who is of course one of today's most distinguished exponents of the Austrian School. Back in 1967, in assessing the comparative influence of Chicago School economists *vis-à-vis* their Austrian School counterparts, Kirzner noted the following:

> The price theory that underlies the contributions of the "Chicago" writers is not fundamentally different from that accepted by American economists generally, including those holding the efficiency and justice

---

[4]See, for instance, Harberger (1988) and Harberger (1993).

of the market system in deep mistrust. It is merely that the "Chicago" economists apply their price theory more consistently and more resolutely, assigning to it a scope of relevance far wider than that granted by others .... "Chicago" price theory, like that taught in most United States economics departments, is solidly in the Anglo-American neo-classical tradition associated most importantly with Alfred Marshall (Kirzner, 1967, p. 102).

To use a bit of economic jargon, one might even say that Harberger, in using the language of neo-classical economics, had a "comparative advantage" in communicating with other economists, as compared to Mises and Hayek, whose Austrian School background seems much more alien to other members of the profession.

There is one other factor I would like to mention, that I also believe is important in explaining Alito's success in communicating with policy makers, and I'm not sure how I should phrase this. Again, I have to confess that I don't know him well, so I'm really sort of guessing here, but from what I can glean from his writings and his public pronouncements, the impression I have is that Alito, for a libertarian, is not a very ideological person. And there is one particular aspect of this that I want to stress here, and it is that if you want to influence economic policy you have to be able to get along with government officials and public sector economists. And you won't be able to do that if you always view them as the enemy.

So I am pretty sure that one important factor that explains Alito's success in public policy reform is that he gets along very well with people in the public sector. He has been a consultant to governments in many countries, and many of his former students have been high-level government officials in their own countries—most notably in Chile, of course, but in many other countries as well. Indeed, Alito often brags about the number of his former students that are or have been ministers of finance, or central bank presidents.[5] He also has many former students in the major international institutions, such as the World Bank and the IMF, and also in the US Agency for International Development.

Let me just end by saying that throughout his long career Arnold Harberger has been a tremendous force for good, and that the world would be a much better place if there were many more economists like him.

Thank you very much.

---

[5]See, for instance, Levy (1999) and Mansell-Carstens (2003).

REFERENCES

Fontaine, Ernesto. 2009. *Mi visión sobre la influencia del Convenio U. Católica – U. de Chicago en el progreso económico y social de Chile*. Foreword by Arnold C. Harberger. Santiago, Chile: Instituto Democracia y Mercado.

Harberger, Arnold C. 1963. "The Dynamics of Inflation in Chile," in C. F. Christ, *et al.*, *Measurement in Economics: Studies in Mathematical Economics and Econometrics in Memory of Yehuda Grunfeld*, pp. 219-50. Stanford, CA: Stanford University Press.

————. 1981. "In Step and Out of Step with the World Inflation: A Summary History of Countries, 1952-76," in Assaf Razin and M. June Flanders (eds.), *Development in an Inflationary World*, pp. 35-46. New York: Academic Press.

————. 1984. (ed.) *World Economic Growth*. San Francisco, CA: ICS Press.

————. 1987. "Reflections on Social Project Evaluation," in Gerald M. Meier (ed.), *Pioneers in Development* (Second Series), pp. 138-47. New York: Oxford University Press.

————. 1988. "El economista y el mundo real: Discurso pronunciado con ocasión de haber sido distinguido con el grado de Doctor Honoris Causa," *Cuadernos de Economía*, 25 (74): 9-26. (English version: *The Economist and the Real World*. Occasional Papers No. 13. San Francisco, CA: International Center for Economic Growth, 1989.)

————. 1993. "The Search for Relevance in Economics," *American Economic Review*, 83 (2): 1-16. (Spanish version: "La búsqueda de relevancia en la economía," *Estudios Públicos*, No. 55 [1994]: 87-114.)

————. 1994. "Notes on Some Issues in Social Project Evaluation," *Journal of International Development*, 6 (1): 95-107.

————. 2003. "Some Recent Advances in Economic Project Evaluation," *Latin American Journal of Economics*, 40 (121): 579-88.

Hines, James R. 2001. "Applied Public Finance Meets General Equilibrium: The Research Contributions of Arnold Harberger," *Proceedings of the Annual Conference on Taxation and Minutes of the Annual Meeting of the National Tax Association*, 94: 1-8.

Kirzner, Israel M. 1967. "Divergent Approaches in Libertarian Economic Thought," *Intercollegiate Review*, 3 (3): 101-08.

Levy, David. 1999. "Interview with Arnold Harberger," *The Region Mazgazine* (Federal Reserve Bank of Minneapolis), 13 (1): 18-21, 36-40.

Mansell-Carstens, Catherine. 2003. "Interview with Arnold C. Harberger," *Economía Mexicana*, 12 (2): 337-66.

Meier, Gerald M. 2001. "The Old Generation of Development Economists and the New," in Gerald M. Meier and Joseph Stiglitz (eds.), *Frontiers of Development Economics*, pp. 13-50. New York: Oxford University Press.

Publications by Julio H. Cole

La metodología del análisis económico. *Revista de la Universidad G. R. Moreno*, No. 39-40 (1985): 30-45.

La inflación como problema contable. *Auditoría y Finanzas*, No. 54 (1985): 5-11.

Inflación en un país pequeño: El caso de Bolivia. *Revista Occidental*, 2 (2-3) (1985): 167-88.

Brother, Can You Spare a Sack of Money? *Reason Magazine*, 17 (8) (1986): 33-35.

Inflation in Latin America, 1970-1980. *Government and Policy*, 4 (1) 1986): 31-41.

Imports and Domestic Inflation in Latin America. *University of South Carolina Studies in Economic Analysis*, 10 (1) (1986): 72-78.

The Terms of Trade Debate: A Critical Review. *Análisis Económico*, 1 (1) 1986): 65-77.

The False Promise of Protectionism for Latin America. *Journal of Economic Growth*, 1 (4) (1986): 28-37.

Inflación en América Latina, 1970-1980. *Acta Academica*, No. 1 (1987): 117-26.

The Latin American Money Game. *New World—A Journal of Latin American Studies*, 2 (1) (1987): 7-11.

Latin American Inflation: Theoretical Interpretations and Empirical Results. New York: Praeger, 1987.

(with MANUEL F. AYAU) Perestroika: Can It Work? *The Freeman*, 38 (12) (1988): 494-95.

The Writings of Adam Smith. *The Freeman*, 40 (2) (1990): 44-46. Reprinted in ANDRÉS MARROQUÍN (ed.), *Invisible Hand: The Wealth of Adam Smith* (Honolulu: University Press of the Pacific, 2002), pp. 5-11.

Adam Smith (1723-1790). *Tópicos de Actualidad*, No. 697 (1990): 20-27.

Review of *Federal Support of Higher Education*, edited by R. E. MEINERS and R. C. AMACHER. *The Freeman*, 40 (6) (1990): 239-40.

La teoría del crecimiento económico en Adam Smith. *Acta Academica*, No. 10 (1992): 57-62.

La obra científica de Friedman. *Libertas,* No. 16 (1992): 39-62.

Dinero y banca. Foreword by MANUEL F. AYAU. México: Editorial Diana, 1992.

Inflación y masa monetaria en Guatemala. *Banca Central*, No. 16 (1993): 40-53.

El modelo smithiano. *Tópicos de Actualidad*, No. 780 (1993): 91-99.

Capital y crecimiento económico. In MANUEL F. AYAU, *El proceso económico*, pp. 8-14 to 8-17. México: Editorial Diana, 1994.

Adam Smith: Economista y filósofo. *Laissez-Faire*, No. 2 (1995): 32-51.

Dinero y banca, 2nd ed. Guatemala: Editorial IDEA, 1995.

Review of *Education and the State*, by E. G. WEST. *The Freeman*, 45 (5) (1995): 334-35.

Elementos de econometría aplicada. Guatemala: Universidad Francisco Marroquín, 1996.

Política monetaria en Guatemala desde 1985. In FRIDOLIN BIRK (ed.), *Guatemala: ¿Oprimida, pobre o princesa embrujada?*, pp. 291-311. Guatemala: Fundación Friedrich Ebert, 1997.

Inflación en Guatemala, 1961-95. *Banca Central*, No. 32 (1997): 21-25. Reprinted in *Revista de Humanidades y Ciencias Sociales*, 3 (1) (1997): 55-62.

¿Se justifican las patentes en una economía libre? *Revista de Humanidades y Ciencias Sociales*, 4 (1) (1998): 87-108. Reprinted, with slight revisions, in *Laissez-Faire*, No. 9 (1998): 47-60 and in *Revista de la Facultad de Derecho* (Universidad Francisco Marroquín), No. 16 (1998): 85-94. Abridged version: *Tópicos de Actualidad*, No. 843 (1998): 63-71.

William Harold Hutt (1899-1988). *Revista de la Facultad de Derecho* (Universidad Francisco Marroquín), No. 18 (2000): 7-10.

Foreword to *Cien obras, mil años*, by ARMANDO DE LA TORRE *et al.* Guatemala: Amigos de la Biblioteca Ludwig von Mises, 2000.

Patentes: Costos y beneficios. *Laissez-Faire*, No. 12-13 (2000): 21-34. Reprinted in *Revista de Humanidades y Ciencias Sociales*, 5 (2) (1999): 23-47 and in *Revista de la Facultad de Derecho* (Universidad Francisco Marroquín), No. 19 (2001): 75-86.

Controversy: Would the Absence of Copyright Laws Significantly Affect the Quality and Quantity of Literary Output? *Journal of Markets and Morality*, 4 (1) (2001): 112-19.

A Response to Paul A. Cleveland. *Journal of Markets and Morality*, 4 (1) (2001): 127-31.

Patents and Copyrights: Do the Benefits Exceed the Costs? *Journal of Libertarian Studies*, 15 (4) (2001): 79-105. Spanish version: *Libertas*, No. 36 (2002): 103-42.

Hayek y la justicia social: Una apreciación crítica. *Laissez-Faire*, No. 16-17 (2002): 51-72. Reprinted in *Revista de Humanidades y Ciencias Sociales*, 7 (1-2) (2001): 1-36 and in *Revista de la Facultad de Derecho* (Universidad Francisco Marroquín), No. 21 (2002): 79-94.

Propiedad intelectual: Comentarios sobre algunas tendencias recientes. *Revista Empresa y Humanismo*, 6 (1) (2003): 35-48. Reprinted in *Anuario Andino de Derechos Intelectuales*, 2 (2005): 313-23.

The Contribution of Economic Freedom to World Economic Growth, 1980-99. *Cato Journal*, 23 (2) (2003): 189-98.

Determinantes del crecimiento económico mundial, 1980-99. *Ciencias Económicas*, 24 (1) (2004): 29-48.

Libertad económica y crecimiento económico mundial, 1980-1999. *Revista de Humanidades y Ciencias Sociales*, 10 (1-2) (2004): 233-50. Reprinted in *Libertas*, No. 42 (2005): 129-49.

La metodología del análisis económico y otros ensayos. Madrid: Unión Editorial, 2004.

Review of *Just Get Out of the Way: How Government Can Help Business in Poor Countries*, by R. E. ANDERSON. *Independent Review*, 9 (3) (2005): 454-56.

Libertad económica y crecimiento económico mundial: Evidencia e implicaciones. In ANDRÉS ROEMER (ed.), *Felicidad: Un enfoque de derecho y economía*, pp. 137-60. México: Universidad Nacional Autónoma de México, 2005. English version: *Revista Latinoamericana de Desarrollo Económico*, No. 5 (2005): 101-23.

Review of *The Collected Works of Arthur Seldon*, vol. 1: *The Virtues of Capitalism*, edited by COLIN ROBINSON. *Journal of Markets and Morality*, 8 (2) (2005): 547-49.

On Eponymy in Economics. *Independent Review*, 11 (1) (2006): 121-31.

Elementos de econometría aplicada, 2nd ed. Guatemala: Universidad Francisco Marroquín, 2006.

(with ROBERT A. LAWSON) Handling Economic Freedom in Growth Regressions: Suggestions for Clarification. *Econ Journal Watch*, 4 (1) (2007): 71-78.

Milton Friedman (1912-2006). *Laissez-Faire*, No. 26-27 (2007): 9-22. Reprinted in *Revista de Economía y Derecho*, 4 (14) (2007): 7-16, in *Revista de Humanidades y Ciencias Sociales*, 12 (1-2) (2006): 221-42 and in *Revista Latinoamericana de Desarrollo Económico*, No. 9 (2007): 155-174. English version: *Independent Review*, 12 (1) (2007): 115-28.

Review of *Milton Friedman: A Biography*, by LANNY EBENSTEIN. *Journal of Markets and Morality*, 10 (2) (2007): 422-25.

Milton Friedman on Income Inequality. *Journal of Markets and Morality*, 11 (2) (2008): 239-53.

Foreword to *Ensayos de historia económica*, by GUSTAVO A. PRADO ROBLES. Ensayos del Instituto de Investigaciones Económicas y Sociales "José Ortíz Mercado", vol. 3. Santa Cruz, Bolivia: Universidad Autónoma Gabriel René Moreno, 2008.

Review of *Patent Failure*, by JAMES BESSEN and MICHAEL J. MEURER. *Independent Review*, 13 (4) (2009): 614-17.

Mario Vargas Llosa: Una travesía intelectual. *Revista de Economía y Derecho*, 6 (24) (2009): 7-15. Reprinted in *Revista de Humanidades y Ciencias Sociales*, 15 (1-2) (2009): 69-78.

(with ANDRÉS MARROQUÍN) Homicide Rates in a Cross-Section of Countries: Evidence and Interpretations. *Population and Development Review*, 35 (4) (2009): 749-76.

Review of *Wellsprings*, by MARIO VARGAS LLOSA. *Independent Review*, 14 (4) (2010): 619-22.

Updating a Classic: "The Poisson Distribution and the Supreme Court" Revisited. *Teaching Statistics*, 32 (3) (2010): 78-80.

Review of *The Global Governance of Knowledge: Patent Offices and Their Clients*, by PETER DRAHOS. *Prometheus*, 29 (1) (2011): 51-54.

Mario Vargas Llosa: An Intellectual Journey. *Independent Review*, 16 (1) (2011): 5-14.

In Memoriam: Joseph E. Keckeissen, 1925-2011. *Laissez-Faire*, No. 35 (2011): 83-85. Reprinted in MARIO ŠILAR (ed.), *Una vida santa dedicada a la libertad: Ensayos en honor de Joe Keckeissen* (Buenos Aires: Instituto Acton Argentina, 2013), pp. 241-46.

Review of *Milton Friedman*, by WILLIAM RUGER. *Journal of Markets and Morality*, 14 (2) (2011): 599-601.

Review of *Innovation and Economic Development: The Impact of Information and Communication Technologies in Latin America*, edited by MARIO CIMOLI, ANDRÉ A. HOFMAN and NANNO MULDER. *Prometheus*, 30 (3) (2012): 315-18.

Milton Friedman: A Bibliography. *Laissez-Faire*, No. 36-37 (2012): 97-122.

Milton Friedman y la Escuela de Chicago. In ADRIÁN O. RAVIER (ed.), *Lecturas de historia del pensamiento económico*, pp. 283-99. Madrid: Unión Editorial, 2012.

Cruzando el umbral de la sociedad abierta: Ideología y libertad en las primeras novelas de Mario Vargas Llosa. In SERGIO SARMIENTO (ed.), *Sexto Concurso de Ensayo Caminos de la Libertad: Memorias*, pp. 27-49. México: Fomento Cultural Grupo Salinas, 2012. Reprinted in

Revista de Humanidades y Ciencias Sociales, 17 (1-2) (2013): 45-71 and in *Ideas & Debate*, No. 5 (2012): 89-116.

Recordando a "Joe Keck". *Revista Areté,* No. 5 (2012): 95-97.

Elementos de econometría aplicada, 3rd ed. Guatemala: J & G Ediciones, 2014.

(with ANDRÉS MARROQUÍN) Economical Writing (or, "Think Hemingway"). *Scientometrics*, 103 (1) (2015): 251-59.

George Orwell y su relevancia para el siglo XXI. In SERGIO SARMIENTO (ed.), *Noveno Concurso de Ensayo Caminos de la Libertad: Memorias*, pp. 66-100. México: Fomento Cultural Grupo Salinas, 2015. Reprinted in *Laissez-Faire*, No. 44-45 (2016): 43-68.

Cinco pensadores liberales. Foreword by MARCO ANTONIO DEL RÍO. Madrid: Unión Editorial, 2016.

Sobre utopías y distopías (con comentarios sobre una novela distópica moderna). *Percontari*, 3 (11) (2016): 13-21. Reprinted in *Laissez-Faire*, No. 47 (2017): 7-18 and in WENCESLAO GIMÉNEZ-BONET and ANTÓN A. TOURSINOV (eds.), *Libertad y convicciones: Ensayos en honor al Dr. Juan Carlos Cachanosky* (Guatemala: Editorial Episteme, 2017), pp. 199-217.

(ed.) *A Companion to Adam Smith*. Guatemala: Universidad Francisco Marroquín, 2017.

www.ingramcontent.com/pod-product-compliance
Lightning Source LLC
Chambersburg PA
CBHW020203200326
41521CB00005BA/235